Realism and Educational Research

Educational research has recently been under attack for being obtuse and irrelevant to the real concerns of practitioners and for making bold claims which it cannot sustain. In this timely book David Scott revisits the roots of educational research.

The first part of the book critiques traditional perspectives on knowledge and educational research and develops a realist framework as an alternative. It addresses issues such as: objectivity, the theory–practice relationship and mathematical modelling. The second part explores a series of controversial debates which have taken place in the field of education including school effectiveness, race and post-modernism.

Realism and Educational Research examines the complex issue of power in educational settings, making reference to the research community itself. It focuses on the way educational research is now being technicised and educational researchers made accountable using evaluative methods which trivialise and distort their findings. This text should prove invaluable for the educational research community, students and educational policy makers.

David Scott is a senior lecturer in curriculum at the Open University and the editor of *The Curriculum Journal*. He has previously worked in the field of educational research at the universities of Warwick, Southampton and London. He has edited *Understanding Educational Research* with Robin Usher published by Routledge and is currently writing a book on how to read educational research and policy reports to be published by RoutledgeFalmer.

D1417005

Social Research and Educational Studies Series

Series Editor: Professor Robert G. Burgess, Vice-Chancellor, University of Leicester

Realism and Educational Research

New Perspectives and Possibilities

David Scott

London and New York

First published 2000 by RoutledgeFalmer
11 New Fetter Lane, London EC4P 4EE

Simultaneously published in the USA and Canada
by RoutledgeFalmer
29 West 35th Street, New York, NY 10001

RoutledgeFalmer is an imprint of the Taylor & Francis Group

© 2000 David Scott

Typeset in Times by
BC Typesetting, Bristol
Printed and bound in Great Britain by
MPG Books Ltd, Bodmin, Cornwall

British Library Cataloguing in Publication Data
A catalogue record for this book is available from the British Library

Library of Congress Cataloguing in Publication Data
Scott, David, 1951–
    Realism and educational research: new perspectives and possibilities/David Scott.
        p.   cm. – (Social research and educational studies series; 19)
    Includes bibliographical references (p.) and indexes.
        1. Education–Research–Philosophy.   2. Education–Research–Methodology.   3.
    Postmodernism and education.   I. Title.   II. Series.
    LB1028.S34 2000
    370'.7'2–dc21   99-054682

ISBN 0 750 70919 7 (hbk)
ISBN 0 750 70918 9 (pbk)

Contents

Contents

Series Editor's Preface

The purpose of the *Social Research and Educational Studies* series is to provide authoritative guides to key issues in educational research. The series includes overviews of fields, guidance on good practice and discussions of the practical implications of social and educational research. In particular, the series deals with a variety of approaches to conducting social and educational research. Contributors to the series review recent work, raise critical concerns that are particular to the field of education and reflect on the implications of research for educational policy and practice.

Each volume in the series draws on material that will be relevant for an international audience. The contributors to this series all have wide experience of teaching, conducting and using educational research. The volumes are written so that they will appeal to a wide audience of students, teachers and researchers. Altogether the volumes in the *Social Research and Educational Studies* series provide a comprehensive guide for anyone concerned with contemporary educational research.

The series includes individually authored books and edited volumes on a range of themes in education including qualitative research, survey research, the interpretation of data, self-evaluation, research and social policy, analysing data, action research and the politics and ethics of research.

Although the literature of social research covers a vast range of material, there has been little on the role of social theory in educational research. In this respect, David Scott's book covers an important gap as it focuses on the centrality of social theory in a variety of empirical projects. The volume covers a range of conceptual and theoretical discussions and subsequently applies these concepts to our analysis of empirical studies. As a consequence it is a volume that deserves to be widely read by students and researchers.

Robert G. Burgess
University of Leicester

Acknowledgements

Parts of Chapters 4, 5, 7, 8 and 10 originally appeared in Scott (1994b), Scott (1996), Scott (1997), Scott (1998), Scott (1999) and Scott and Usher (1999). Each of these extracts has been significantly revised. Permission to use this material has been given by the London Institute of Education, Cassell, Taylor and Francis (*Journal of Education Policy*), Stanley Thornes (Publishers) Ltd. and Falmer Press.

This book is dedicated with thanks and love to Moira, Sarah and Ben.

1 Introduction

This book is intended to fill a gap in the literature of educational research. It aims to find an alternative to mathematical modelling and its unconsidered empiricist underpinnings on the one hand and hermeneutic or interpretive frameworks on the other. It is unashamedly realist, albeit in a transcendental sense. Roy Bhaskar (1979, p. ix), writing twenty years ago, suggested that 'both the dominant naturalist tradition, positivism, and its naturalistic hermeneutical foil rest on an ontology rendered obsolete by new collateral theories of philosophy and ideology. The time is therefore overdue for a "sublation" of their historic confrontation.' Since then little has changed, except that, in the field of education, the dominant ideology of positivism/empiricism has become perhaps even more dominant. New developments in statistical methods have led some (cf. Goldstein, 1998) to suggest that the criticisms addressed at mathematical modelling, ie. its reductive and trivialising orientation, can finally be overcome.[1] At the bridgehead between two millennia, this increasingly seems to reflect hope rather than achievement. Furthermore, educational research has been recently subject to a number of trenchant criticisms, from both within (cf. Hargreaves, 1996a; Tooley with Darby, 1998[2]) and outside (cf. Woodhead, 1998; Barber, 1996). These criticisms have centred on its obtuseness, its irrelevance to the real concerns of practitioners and, even more so, its boldness in making claims which it cannot sustain. Hargreaves (1996b, p. 7), for example, suggests that there is a considerable amount of 'frankly second rate educational research which does not make a serious contribution to fundamental theory or knowledge; which is irrelevant to practice; which is uncoordinated with any preceding or follow-up research; and which clutters up academic journals that virtually nobody reads'. It is therefore appropriate to revisit its roots; to examine how it is possible to research educational activities and environments.

The book will make reference to some common fallacies in educational research. These are:

Introduction

1 *The epistemic fallacy* – Ontology and epistemology are conflated so that it is not possible to understand how transitive methods may be used to examine relatively intransitive structures.

2 *The fallacy of homogeneity* – The characteristics given to a group of people are assumed to apply to individuals within that group.

3 *The causal fallacy* – Observed patterns of behaviour are construed as causal configurations.

4 *The essentialist fallacy* – Appearances are frequently conflated with essences and understood as all there is.

5 *The fallacy of value-free knowledge* – Knowledge of educational institutions and systems is thought of as value-free. Educational researchers therefore ignore the value-rich dimension of their activities.

6 *The prospective fallacy* – Retrospective viewpoints are frequently conflated with prospective viewpoints. Educational researchers may be able to explain what has happened, but this does not mean that they know what will happen.

7 *The reductive fallacy* – Human characteristics and attributes are reduced to variables which cannnot be further reduced and which when combined capture the essence of either that human being or the educational activities which they are engaged in. This acts to trivialise and distort descriptions of those activities.

8 *The deterministic fallacy* – Frequently educational researchers neglect human intention and creativity in their descriptions of educational activities.

9 *The fallacy of pragmatism* – Educational researchers understand research as a practical activity which can be carried on without reference to epistemological and ontological concerns.

These nine fallacies will appear and reappear at different points in the argument throughout the book. Indeed, the first part of the book sets out a particular approach to educational research which avoids the pitfalls expressed above.

The second half offers a discussion of methodological disputes in various sub-fields of the discipline. These sub-fields are: school effectiveness, policy, biography/autobiography, race and post-modernism. Each of these is discussed in terms of the framework for educational research developed in the first part, and it is worth setting out here the principles which underpin that framework. These principles[3] are as follows and they are listed in no particular order:

1 Educational research is itself educational. The researcher is as much a learner as those who form the subject matter of the research.

2 There are real objects in the world which do not depend for their existence on whether they are known by anyone or everyone.

3 Of some objects we only have knowledge of their appearances but these make reference to deeper-lying structures.

4 Any claims we make about knowledge are fallible and furthermore embedded within contemporary ways of knowing.

5 There may be occasions when appearances and deep structures conflict.

6 It is possible to understand the process of doing educational research as one of gathering changing knowledge of relatively unchanging entities.

7 Educational researchers are inevitably implicated in the production of knowledge about educational activities and institutions.

8 Educational knowledge is embedded within micro-political systems (indeed, this is both the subject matter of research and its necessary context), which are understood as having weak or strong boundaries between the different parts.

9 The essential ontological relation which educational researchers need to examine is the relationship between structure and agency or enablement and constraint. This relation is expressed, following Archer (1995), as a morphogenetic one.

10 Educational researchers need to examine: real structural properties at each time point; interpretations of those structures by relevant social actors; real relations between different structures at each time point; perceived relations between different structures at each time point by the relevant social actors; the intentions of the players in the game (actors may also be motivated by unconscious forces); the unintended consequences of actions; the subsequent effect of those intended and unintended actions on structural properties; and the degrees of structural influence and agential freedom for each human interaction.

Evaluating Research

The book will also attempt to answer some fundamental questions about research methodology and education. The most important of these is: how do we distinguish good from bad research?[4] Or to put it in another way, what criteria can we use to judge different research methods, approaches and texts?

Various sets of criteria have been developed to allow researchers and readers of research to determine what is good research. Classical sets of criteria referred to the representativeness of the account. Thus an account was judged in terms of its *internal validity* (whether experimentally the effects observed as a result of the intervention were actually caused by it and not by something else); *external validity* (whether findings from the case being investigated could be generalised to other cases in time and place); and *objectivity* (whether the preconceptions and biases of the researcher had been accounted for in the construction of the account and eliminated as influencing variables). Guba and Lincoln (1985) suggested alternative criteria, though these were criticised for not being alternative or radical enough. They were: *credibility* (whether respondents agreed that the researcher has adequately represented their constructions of reality); *transferability* (whether the readers of the research agreed that the conclusions reached related usefully to settings which they themselves were immersed in); *dependability* (whether the researcher had been able to identify his/her effects during fieldwork and discount them); and *confirmability* ('the key question here is whether the data are qualitatively confirmable; in other words, whether the analysis is grounded in the data and whether inferences based on the data are logical and of high utility' (Guba and Lincoln, 1985, p. 323)).

Guba and Lincoln came under fierce attack for grounding this set of criteria within a positivist perspective or rather for espousing a form of realism, albeit not of a naive kind. Certainly they accepted that their set of criteria was underpinned by the idea of a correct method which would lead to the uncovering of reality and that this concentration on method was at the expense of epistemology and ontology. In an attempt to distance themselves from a positivist/empiricist perspective, Guba and Lincoln (1989) developed a further set of criteria: *fairness* (equal consideration should be given to all the various perspectives of participants in the research); *educative authenticity* (good research involves participants in the process of educating themselves); *catalytic authenticity* (this is where the research process has stimulated activity and decision-making); and *empowerment* (participants are now in a better position to make real choices about their professional activity). Hammersley (1992) suggests another four-fold schema: *plausability/credibility* (whether the evidential claims are plausible or credible to the reader of the research); *coherence* (whether evidence and argument logically cohere); *intentionality* (whether a study is credible in terms of its stated intentions); and *relevance* (whether the research findings are relevant to issues of legitimate public concern). Evers and Lakomski (1991), arguing from a position of coherentist realism, suggest that research should be judged by whether it observes the virtues of *simplicity, consistency, coherence, comprehensiveness, conservativeness* and *fecundity*.

There are also post-modernist critiques. Post-modernism is essentially an attack on foundationalism of all kinds and the application of universal criteria in making judgements about research texts. Nevertheless, judgements are made, not least about this book, in all sorts of fora. For post-modernists it is the nature of these judgements which is of concern, rather than the identification of a correct method for their making. Their concern is to understand how these judgements are made, which relations of power they imply and what effects they have. Foucault's (1980) notion of genealogy is directly concerned to do just this: to understand how the reader, be they policy-maker, university reader or practitioner, is positioned in relation to existing arrangements of power. This has been called a transgressive approach to judging research (cf. Scott and Usher, 1999).

These sets of criteria overlap with each other and each in turn places greater emphasis on one of the core principles (representativeness, coherence, action) than on the others. Proponents of each seek to construct an argument based round whether the research:

- is representative;
- corresponds with some external reality;
- is validated by respondents from the research setting which goes beyond affirmation of the truthfulness of events or activities;
- is grounded in the data;
- successfully changes what is;
- is consistent and coherent;
- is relevant in some specified way; or
- surfaces underlying power relations in the research setting and as a consequence repositions players in the game.

Correspondence notions of representation have proved to be problematic; the argument being that language does not function by describing in a neutral way what is, but is both implicated in the construction of that reality and subject to a variety of micro-political processes. Thus definitional truths are only valid in so much as they provide the means for discovering how meanings have been constructed and how those constructions have evolved within the life world of a particular community of knowers.

The Organisation of the Book

Having briefly sketched out some of the main arguments of the book, let me now turn to how it is organised. Chapters 2 and 3 examine the idea of knowing and its companionate concept of education. Understanding is construed, following Gadamer (1975), as never being disinterested. Knowing the world comprises both recognising the parameters of a given situation and of the knower's own possibilities within it. For Gadamer (1975, p. 260), this educative process is a form of self-understanding, so that he can say: 'all such understanding is ultimately self-understanding . . . Thus it is true in every case that a person who understands, understands himself, projecting himself upon his possibilities.' Furthermore, since the act of knowing is educative, then this places an additional burden on the educational researcher. Three versions of truth are identified: naive realism, radical relativism and transcendental realism. The epistemic fallacy is introduced and this serves as a structuring theme for the rest of the book. The framework for educational research introduced in this book has three dimensions: ontological, epistemological and methodological. The onto-logical dimension comprises a relationship between structure and agency; the epistemological dimension identifies the value-embeddedness of the research enterprise; and the methodological dimension, which is derived from the first two, comprises the argument that social research necessarily has to incorporate an ethnographic element.[5]

Chapter 4 offers a series of criticisms of an influential strategy in edu-cational research, mathematical modelling. These comprise: an argument for systematic unpredictability in human affairs; an argument resisting a determinate view of human nature; an argument which suggests that change over time can only be understood qualitatively because educational activities occur within open systems of social relations; an argument in favour of a generative rather than successionist view of causation; and finally, an argument which suggests that because mathematical modelling acts to package the intensional dimension of social life in such a way as to proceed with formal calculations, this reductive act serves to distort and trivialise proper descriptions of educational processes.

Chapter 5 sets out five possible positions educational researchers can take with regards to the relationship between theory and practice. These posi-tions are: technical rationality, technical efficiency, theoretical guidance, non-technicism and theory–practice separation. The chapter ends with an account of a theory of professional development within educational institu-tions which is developed from previous discussion of these five theories. These four chapters, then, set out a theory of educational research. The second part of the book examines five controversies in educational research in the light of the discussion in the first part.

Chapter 6 examines one of the most influential of contemporary educa-tional discourses, school effectiveness. This programme is shown to be flawed. The first problem with it is that the definition of effectiveness which is central to the discourse is a value-rich concept, indeed at every stage of the methodological procedures, values seep in almost unnoticed. This managerial discourse is further shown to have committed itself to a technicist view of education, a behavioural objectives view of curriculum, a behaviourist view of human behaviour, a reductionist methodology which determines how it is viewed and how the discourse is constructed, a marginalisation of debates about the aims and purposes of education and a misunderstanding of the equity debate.

Chapter 7 concentrates on the ontological position taken up in the first part of the book and suggests a way of understanding the policy dimension in education. The key theme of the relationship between structure and agency is shown at work in the way National Curriculum assessment arrangements in the United Kingdom have been formed and reformed over the last fifteen years and how these have impacted on the practice of teachers.

Chapter 8 examines an increasingly important activity in the field, that of biography and auto-biography. This again reprises many of the themes addressed in the first part of the book and suggests a form of enquiry which allows appreciation of the driving force of society: the complex inter-actional activity of individuals and groups of individuals, all seeking to create and recreate themselves in the context of forms of life which are continually undergoing transformation. What is also examined in this chapter is how we can know these activities and this ties closely together auto-biography with biography.

Chapter 9 attempts to mediate between two antagonistic factions in the debates about the impact of race on educational settings. Protagonists of these two factions disagree about whether education should be conceived as racialised, and, more importantly for this book, about how we can know whether it is racialised. These methodological disagreements have deeper roots, and on the one side is a suggestion that all research has a critical dimension, whilst the other would want to argue that partisanship in educational research defeats its own objectives.

The tenth chapter examines the influence of post-modern thinking on educational research and in particular some of the themes that occur and recur in the work of the French philosopher, Michel Foucault. Some of these themes are epistemological, ie. whether trans-epistemic knowledge is possible; and some are ontological, ie. how people and populations are controlled in modern societies. It is appropriate to conclude Part 2 in this way because of the impact his thinking has had on the discourse of education.

The final chapter offers a way forward for those engaged in answering the question: how should we proceed as educational researchers? It does attempt to grapple with the complex issue of power in educational research settings, since much of the methodological literature is fundamentally concerned with this. It also makes reference to the research community itself and the way educational research is now being technicised and educational researchers made accountable using evaluative methods which trivialise and distort its purpose and products. The Research Assessment Exercise for United Kingdom Universities and the increasing use of systems for quantifying research output are examples of this. The need therefore for a properly argued defence of educational research has never been more timely.

Part 1

Theorising Educational Research

2 The Contested Nature of Educational Research

Three Versions of Truth

The field of education is riven with disputes, not least about the veracity of different research approaches. These are usually conducted at the level of method and strategy with little attention paid to epistemology and ontology. And yet it is only at these levels that the real issues are foremost. Epistemology focuses on knowledge, ontology on the reality which we seek to know. It is the relationship between the two which is central to the discussion in this chapter. It is possible to identify three broadly conceived positions in relation to these debates: naive realism, radical relativism and transcendental realism.

Naive realism is underpinned by a social theory known as positivism and a philosophical theory known as empiricism. Kolakowski (1972) suggests that a positivistic model should include four separate elements: phenomenalism, nominalism, a distinction between facts and values, and the unity of the scientific method. The first of these, phenomenalism, refers to the idea that social scientists should only be concerned with surface phenomena and not with underlying essences. Both natural and social scientists should therefore concentrate on how these surface and observable phenomena manifest themselves in regular patterns. The second element is nominalism. This refers to the belief that the world consists of social and physical facts which cannot be further reduced in any way. The researcher's task is to identify those facts which exist by virtue of what the world is and they exist prior to their perception or conceptualisation by social actors. Researchers therefore bracket out their value systems and discover what is, and their accounts as a result correspond with that reality in a straightforward way.

The third element comprises the separation of factual from value statements and is a logical extension of nominalism. Kolakowski (1972, p. 13) argues that: 'the phenomenalist, nominalist conception of science has another important consequence, namely, the rule that refuses to call value judgements and normative statements knowledge'. An extreme version of this doctrine can be found in the philosophy of logical positivism (cf. Ayer, 1954), advocates of which argue that value-impregnated statements cannot qualify as scientific accounts of the world and that aesthetic, ethical and religious statements are of this order. However, it is still possible to make a number of statements about the world, shorn of values, which reflect the world as it is and are not dependent on the personal viewpoint of the knower. The fourth element comprises a unity of method. Natural and social scientific researchers should use the same criteria to judge their activities and behave in all essential respects the same way. Method is designated as universal – there is only one correct way of understanding social and natural phenomena. Advocates of this model therefore make law-like or nomothetic statements about the world and their methods allow replicability. These general laws comprise 'the constant conjunction of atomistic events or states of affairs, interpreted as the objects of actual or possible experience' (Bhaskar, 1979, p. 158).

Empiricism, on the other hand, may be characterised in the following way: knowledge of the world comes from the senses; the brain is passively imprinted on with that knowledge and has no ordering role; the motion is individualistic in that it does not depend on anyone else's experience of the same phenomenon; it is atomistic in that each experience can be understood as it is and without reference to other experiences; and these experiences are successive in time and combined (though we may experience patterns or constant conjunctions of these atomistic experiences). Both positivism and empiricism have been challenged in the twentieth century; indeed, the problem increasingly has become one of defining what these two terms mean.[6] This does not, however, preclude us from examining ideal models of both and suggesting an alternative which better meshes with new developments in philosophy and social theory.

The first criticism which has been made concerns the proposed relationship between epistemology and ontology. For empiricists the epistemological given is deemed to represent reality; that is, epistemology and ontology are conflated. What is given to our senses, when our senses are cleansed of any notion of preconception, constitutes the world as it is. The world is not constructed by and through us, or to be more accurate, by and through communities of knowers. Language is understood as a neutral medium. In opposition to this, it has been suggested that sense data are always received in terms of a conceptual schema which makes sense of them. The observer is therefore not a passive receiver, but an active mediator of knowledge of events. The mind engages in creative work on and in the world. Furthermore, this is a worldly production, that is, the mind works in the world in a public sense and our theories about the world are always historically specific and dependent on communities of knowers producing knowledge. Empiricism denies the possibility of genuine disagreement about events or human activities. However, genuine disagreement does not rest on mistaken impression, because if it did we could quickly resolve our differences. Genuine disagreement rests on different ways of ordering the world, which may make reference to data but is never determined by them.

Empiricists also suggest that since data are passively received, each individual processes the same data in the same way (that is, because we passively receive data, the sameness must inhere in the sense impression, as therefore does its meaning) without reference to the way it is communicated to other human beings receiving the same impressions. In addition, the theory is underpinned by a successionist rather than a generative theory of causality. Because of the atomism at the heart of empiricism, each event is treated in isolation, and because of the notion of constant conjunction, each series of events implies that each of them is equivalent. Generative theories of causation separate out structures, which generate and have the potential to generate successive occurrences, from those events or occurrences. What this means is that the empiricist deals with the manifestations of mechanisms and not with real objects in the world. Empiricists embrace a form of naive realism which conflates thought and reality in a particular way. Sayer (1992, p. 47), for instance, argues that:

> The illusion of the appeal to facts in popular discourse involves collapsing statements into their referents, thought objects into real objects. It thereby appears to appeal to the facts themselves, the way the world is, in an unmediated fashion, but it is actually an appeal to a particular way of talking about the world in some conceptual system, and therefore may be contested.

Naive realism can be compared with another doctrine, radical relativism. Here the principle is that the world or reality does not and cannot exert a specific influence on the mind. In short, it is up to us as to how we see the world. And what follows from this is that by substituting one conceptual frame for another, we literally change the world. The theories we have are not just underdetermined by data from the world, they are not determined at all; and this implies that it is not possible to develop criteria by which we can judge one version against another. All versions of the truth are equally valid. Objects of discourse do not exist as such, because all we have is the discourse or the discourse expressed as text. Again what follows from this version of superidealism, as Bhaskar (1989) calls it, is that each mind creates its own world without reference to the way other minds create their worlds.

In short, observational data are never considered to be theory-neutral, but always mediated through structures, paradigms and world views. Furthermore, these latter are not just epistemological frameworks but normative beliefs about how the researcher would like the world to be. The implication of this is that no one framework is superior to another and that we simply have to live with such value disagreements. The way we therefore settle disputes is practical, by the exercise of power, whereby those with greater control of allocative (material features of the environment and the means of material production and reproduction) and authoritative (the organisation of time–space, the body and life-chances in society) resources (Giddens, 1984) impose their view on the world. Radical relativism implies an unbreakable conflation of thought and reality. Indeed, it challenges the distinction between statements and referents and implies that statements only refer to other statements and not to any underlying reality. Whereas radical relativism collapses reality into text, naive objectivism does the same but in reverse order, collapsing text into reality (Sayer, 1992).

There are a number of middle positions which do not involve a conflation of the two. One of these is transcendental realism developed by Bhaskar (1979) amongst others. A distinction is made between ontology (being) and epistemology (knowing) so that to conflate the two becomes illegitimate – the epistemic fallacy. Epistemology is always transitive, and therefore subject to the prevailing power arrangements in society. Ontology, however, certainly with regards to the social sciences, is relatively enduring: 'Once we constitute an intransitive dimension, we can see how changing knowledge of unchanging objects is possible' (Bhaskar, 1979, p. 11).[7] However, the relationship between the two is far from straightforward. Bhaskar identifies four foundational principles: there are objects in the world whether they are known or not; knowledge is fallible because any claim to knowledge may be open to refutation; there are transphenomenalist truths in which one may only have knowledge of what appears, but these refer to underlying structures which are not easily apprehended; most importantly, there are counter-phenomenalist truths in which those deep structures may actually contradict or be in conflict with their appearances.

To conflate epistemological and ontological concerns, as empiricists do, is to mistake the experience of the constant conjunctions of events for the causal mechanisms which underpin them. Bhaskar, as a realist, separates out the three domains of the *real* (consisting of mechanisms), the *actual* (consisting of events) and the *empirical* (consisting of experiences) and argues that relations between them are contingent. Events can occur in the world without them being observed by everyone or indeed by anyone; mechanisms can act to neutralise other mechanisms, so that nothing changes in life which can be directly observed; indeed, mechanisms may not be activated but still retain their potential powers to influence events.

Empiricists conflate the knowing of the world with what it is. This is implicit in the unproblematic nature of representation which they espouse. Epistemology as such is bypassed and they move without thought to the reality they seek to express. Idealists are involved in a further bypassing, but this time of reality, in that epistemology is all there is. The consequence of accepting the epistemic fallacy is that epistemology and ontology are separated at least conceptually, or, as Bhaskar's version suggests, conflating the two in various ways is deemed to be illegitimate. Ontology or being in the world is therefore designated as a separate activity from our knowledge of it or its epistemology. Collier (1994, pp. 76–77) suggests a number of ways in which the epistemic fallacy is manifested:

1) the question whether something exists gets reduced to the question whether we can know that it exists; 2) the question what sort of thing something is gets reduced to the question how we can know about it; 3) the question whether A has causal/ontological primacy over B gets reduced to the question whether knowledge of A is presupposed by knowledge of B; 4) the question whether A is identical to B gets reduced to the question whether our way of knowing A is identical to our way of knowing B.

These four different versions of the epistemic fallacy are different in significant ways, though they are all legitimate versions of it. They express different relations: those of existence, identity, causality and equivalence.

To translate this highly abstract schema into the language of research requires us to identify some common mistakes in the field of education. One such mistake is to conflate correlations with causes. If *a* correlates with *b* (given an acknowledged degree of probability), then it is possible to conclude that *a* caused *b* to happen. However, the existence of perverse correlations (cf. Scott, 1999)[8] would seem to indicate that there are problems, and it is possible to suggest that a mistake has occurred because the two variables have been misconceived; or because they refer to surface phenomena and neglect underlying mechanisms; or because they assume an equivalence across cases which is not justified; or because they confuse cause and consequence; or for a host of other reasons.

An example of this is Levine and Lezotte's (1990) assertion that school effectiveness is enhanced by 'vigorous selection and replacement of teachers'. It is assumed that the selection process which is described here as vigorous, indicating either that it is extensive or that it is carried out with enthusiasm, has resulted in one set of teachers who were not considered to be good enough, ie. were not instrumental in children's learning when that learning correlated with improved examination results, being replaced by another set of teachers who were more effective in doing this. However, there is another possibility, which is that the act of culling a set of teachers (however it was achieved and it is possible to make the assumption that it was achieved in different ways in the schools which comprised the sample) had the effect of indicating to those teachers who remained that they should work in a particular way (it would also be perverse not to expect newly recruited teachers to understand what was going on), and that this is what caused the improvement in examination results. Now, the identification of the causal sequence (which may be different in the different schools in the sample) has been obscured because of the need to express that causal mechanism in a way that allows the two variables to be correlated (ie. the variable itself has to be equivalent to other instances of it in all essential respects) and this means that a perverse relationship may have been established. The question of whether there is a causal relationship between the actions of head teachers and their replacement and recruitment of staff is reduced to the question of how we can know it.

Another common fallacy in educational research is to claim that what practitioners say they did is the same as what actually happened. Sammons et al.'s (1997) study of effective school departments infers the existence of successful mechanisms for school improvement from interviews conducted with head teachers and heads of department, who, it could be suggested, understand the clear need to talk about their school practices in terms of a discourse of school effectiveness. If we want to treat epistemology and ontology as separate, then we have to address three questions. What is the nature of the reality which we are attempting to find out about? How can we know it? And what are the implications of answers to these first two questions for our choice of methods if we engage in empirical research? The first of these which will be addressed is the epistemological dimension.

Objectivity

The matter of objectivity is of crucial importance to the study of education. However, before we say why, it is necessary to distinguish between the different ways this term is used. Has it simply become a synonym for the truth of the matter? Does it refer to a particular method of enquiry which if properly carried out guarantees access to truthful accounts of the world? The term has become one of those essentially contested concepts.[9] It is used in a number of ways.

Firstly, it may be used to indicate that a description of the world about which a claim of validity is being made is accurate. Under this definition a relativist could make the claim that their description of the world is objective because all they mean by this is that it is true (they may of course define truth in a way which is unacceptable to some people). If the claims of relativism can be shown to be necessary truths, then a further claim, under this definition, could be made which is that they are also objective. The word itself is used in such a way that it is given little real work to do, because it has become a synonym for 'truth'.

The second way objectivity is defined is when it refers to the use of a particular way of conducting an empirical enquiry. The data collector is understood as free of bias and therefore objective if they act without prejudice. Bias may be understood in a variety of ways, but to define it simply as free of those activities and dispositions which act to conceal the truth is of course tautological. What has to be identified is those dispositions of the data collector which lead to untruthful accounts emerging. These have been construed in a number of ways.

There is the possibility of human error. A researcher thinks that they have collected a full range of data, when in fact they have unintentionally ignored parts of it, and this constitutes bias. Or, the researcher has interpreted the data in one possible way and ignored alternative interpretations, not out of any sense of wishing to give one impression rather than another, but from ignorance or laziness or neglect. It can still be considered to be an honest error because there is no intention to bias the account.

There is furthermore what could be called dishonest error. Here, the researcher deliberately ignores data or refuses to collect them because this may lead them to draw conclusions which they do not want to make. Another example of this form of bias would be when the researcher chooses a method for collecting data which is in their opinion not appropriate. This form of bias is relatively easy to understand, but not necessarily to identify from the perspective of the outsider, because it is characterised by a deliberate attempt to incorporate a falsifying element into the proceedings.

Another type of bias may be construed as interest-bound. Interests are defined here in a limited sense, since it could be said that ethical, political, social or religious motivations are also interest-bound. However, there is a difference between these and interests defined in a narrower sense where the individual is rewarded in some specific way, eg. in terms of renumeration, status or advancement, if they fulfil their part of a bargain. Contract researchers clearly have an interest in satisfying the demands of their sponsors and this may include presenting their research in a selective way to fit with the expectations and world-views of those sponsors. Of course, this is never a straightforward process because the researcher may not know in any complete sense what those expectations and world-views are. This model of research or evaluation (and it more frequently applies to evaluators rather than researchers) could be said to be biased, and is sometimes compared with a version of research called 'blue-skies' in which it is argued that bias of this kind is not present. Again it is important to ask the question as to whether any research can be free of interest-related bias since all research when made public has consequences which may act to the detriment or to the advantage of the researcher.

Finally, there is a type of bias which it is more difficult still to explain. This comprises a range of activities which could be considered to be ideological,[10] but which, because they are so central to the belief-systems of individual researchers, cannot be said, on immediate inspection, to be able to be corrected. If we are to sustain a notion of bias, we also have to sustain a notion that it is possible to correct that bias and behave in a less biased or unbiased manner. These belief systems may be religious, political, ethical or social. A catholic researcher examining the use of capital punishment in the United States of America could not, without doing damage to their fundamental beliefs, forego taking up a particular ethical position towards the subject matter of their research. What they hear or see or read is thus always filtered through a particular ideology. A feminist, again, could not and would not want to interpret data in a way which conflicted with their core beliefs. The question which needs to be answered with regards to this form of bias, if we are to construe it as bias, is whether those essential beliefs contribute to a situation which produces a distorted view of reality. In other words, could a researcher bracket out their core beliefs and produce an untainted or uncommitted version of reality? Would this so-called unbiased position simply be another ideological position, albeit that it seeks to conceal (both from itself and from other people) its true nature?

The third sense in which objectivity is used embraces a whole range of meanings and is educative and self-reflexive in nature. It makes reference to the problem we encountered above, which is that political, ethical, social and religious frameworks which structure the activity of the researcher in totalising ways may constitute a form of bias. Is it, in other words, possible to step outside these belief systems and somehow see the world without reference to them?

For Gadamer (1975), this is impossible; indeed, he would want to rescue the term 'bias' from its negative undertones. Instead of seeking to eliminate bias, he would want to embrace it. All understanding, for him, is educative and has to be contextualised in terms of those pre-existing states which the knower finds him- or herself in. Knowledge therefore has a pre-text (Usher, 1997). However, he is also concerned to elaborate the idea that, though researchers and those seeking to educate themselves, do so within familiar contexts, they also have to make sense of the unfamiliar. The process of understanding comprises the incorporation of the strange into the familiar which has the effect of changing what is familiar so that in any future encounters the knower is positioned differently. For Gadamer (1975, p. 125), it is the tension between the strange and the familiar which contributes to the dialectic of research:

> Hermeneutic work is based on a polarity of familiarity and strangeness. There is a tension. It is the play between the traditionary text's strangeness and familiarity to us, between being a historically intended, distanciated object and belonging to a tradition. The true locus of hermeneutics is this in-between.

The continuous interplay between 'the whole', which may be understood as the knower's world-view, and the 'new', which is that which is strange to the knower, is described as a 'hermeneutic circle'. Though we are predisposed to see certain things in certain ways, this should not preclude us from understanding that these ways are continually undergoing transformation because of new encounters with the world. In short, our assumptions are continually being challenged.

The most important implication of this is that knowledge-gathering is never a disinterested activity. Furthermore, it is an exploration of both what is being investigated in the world and the researcher's own sense of possibility within it. Gadamer refers to this as the 'fusion of horizons' and it comprises a radically different way of understanding research. It also involves a reconceptualisation of such concepts as objectivity and bias. We therefore at this point need to address the role and place of values in educational research. Furthermore, we may want to draw certain conclusions from the discussion and these will certainly have implications for the way researchers should behave.

Paradigms of Knowledge

It is perhaps appropriate to begin by referring to the notion of an epistemic paradigm. Kuhn's *The Structure of Scientific Revolutions* (1971) was a seminal book in the philosophy of science and indeed has had a profound influence on the philosophy of the social sciences, a matter of much concern to those interested in developing a social theory of educational knowledge. Kuhn's startling thesis was in opposition to Hacking's (1981) eight theses (actually nine, but two of them have been conflated) which comprised the traditional image of science:

1 *Realist assumptions* – There is a real world out there which does not depend on how it is understood or articulated by any human being. Furthermore, there is a uniquely best way of describing it, which is not dependent on history or society.
2 *Demarcation* – Scientific theories are very different from other types of beliefs.
3 *Cumulative orientation* – Science works by building on previous ideas and theories; indeed, it works towards an ultimate goal, which is a proper understanding of the natural world.
4 *Distinction between observation and theory* – Observational statements and theoretical statements are treated as separate.
5 *Epistemological justification* – Hypotheses and theories are tested deductively by observations and experiments.
6 *Fixity of meaning* – Linguistic terms have fixed meanings and concepts are defined precisely.
7 *Distinction between judgement and procedure* – The production of truthful statements is different from how they are justified.

8 *Unitary method* – Similar methods are appropriate to the discovery of truths about the natural and social worlds.

No single philosophy has embraced all eight points.[11] For example, Popper (1976) rejected the distinction made between observational and theoretical statements.

Kuhn offers a radical critique of these assumptions. Usher (1996, p. 15) shows how Kuhn:

> . . . presents science as a socio-historical practice carried out in research communities within which individual researchers are located. Sometimes the community is fairly invisible; very often (and this tends to be the case in social and educational research) it is fragmented and incoherent . . . Another tendency of positivist/empiricist epistemology is to present science and scientific research as rationalistic. Kuhn on the other hand presents rationality as mediated and shaped by factors such as socialisation, conformity, faith and processes very much akin to religious conversion.

For Kuhn, science is characterised by a sequence of activities: normal science is beset with crises, which in turn lead to revolutions, which in their turn lead to periods of normal science. This is a paradigmatic view in which the paradigm[12] of normal science is protected by important gate-keepers who vet what is considered appropriate knowledge and what is considered appropriate ways of determining truth from falsehood. At a certain point in time normal science is unable to solve pressing anomalies. As Hacking (1981, p. 3) suggests: 'Revolution occurs because new achievements present new ways of looking at things, and then in turn create new problems for people to get on with. Often old problems are shelved or forgotten.' What this means is that different paradigms are incommensurable, because the criteria for what counts as knowledge are literally different for different paradigms. In the social sciences these may be called epistemes (Foucault, 1972) or traditions (Macintyre, 1988). However, advocates for them still have to confront the age-old problem that it is difficult to make a proper judgement about an activity within one paradigm, episteme or tradition from the perspective of another. Any judgements are locked into the paradigm from which they are made. A further consequence is that science loses its cumulative orientation because paradigms are not considered by Kuhn to be in any way superior or inferior to each other (if they were, they would not be paradigms as such, since they could then be arranged in a hierarchical fashion). What this schema also implies is that when a revolution occurs, we see everything from a different perspective. Since the paradigm is essentially an epistemological construction, it affects all our operations and activities in the world.

If we accept the notion of epistemic paradigms, then this may lead us down the path towards relativism. There are three possible routes. The first is to reject the idea of paradigmatic knowledge; the second is to embrace it and therefore understand any knowledge of the world as both speculative and tentative *and* as paradigm-specific; the third, however, is to accept that communities of knowers produce knowledge in particular ways, but this does not and cannot rule out the possibility of transitive and therefore context-dependent knowledge of relatively unchanging objects (however we understand these and transcendental realists understand them in specific ways). If this last is correct, then we need to examine this transitive epistemological dimension.

Value Freedom or Value Relevance

If values (epistemic or otherwise) play a significant part in that activity which we call educational research, then it is important to understand how they do so and in what way. Weber (1974) distinguishes between value-free activities (Wertfreiheit) and value-relevant activities (Wertbeziehung) in social science research. For Weber, the research act comprises three phases. The first is orientation and he concludes that what orientates us to do a piece of research is not and cannot be value-free. Likewise, the third phase, dissemination, cannot be free of values, whether those of researchers, policy-makers or practitioners. However, in the middle phase the researcher should and can be uncommitted. The middle phase comprises activities such as data collection and data analysis. This is indeed the main obstacle to a reconciliation between positivistically inclined researchers and those of a more hermeneutic orientation, with the former arguing for Weber's position and the latter finding even this compromise problematic.

What are the problems with the idea that this middle phase can be value-neutral? First, there seems to be an ideological dimension to knowledge, which is that events in the world are seen differently through different eyes, and that there is no neutral way of resolving those differences. In other words, both or many perspectives are equally valid. The fact may not be as factual as it seems, especially if it is defined as an ontological given about the world which cannot be disputed by any rational observer. An example will bring out the force of this argument. In *School Matters: The Junior Years* (Mortimore et al., 1988), Table 9.1 presents the data collected about the ethnic composition of the sample of pupils in the research (see Table 2.1). Respondents were asked (or the decision was made for them) to define themselves in terms of a number of distinct ethnic categories: these were aggregated into three groups – *Caribbean*, *Asian* and *English/Scottish/Welsh and Irish*. The criterion used was therefore one of biological heritage. Because the parents/grandparents/ancestors of the pupils were born or lived in or were deported to certain parts of the world, it is possible

Table 2.1 Differences between schools in the ethnic composition of first-year pupil intakes

	Asian	Caribbean	English/Scottish Welsh/Irish
Average % all schools	6.8	11.8	59.0
Maximum % pupils any school	37.5	52.6	95.6
Minimum % pupils any school	0	0	22.0

(From Mortimore et al., 1988, p. 177 – Table 9.1)

to classify those pupils in a certain way, and more importantly, as different from those who have been classified in a different way. Their identity – how they understand themselves – is fixed by their parentage, and moreover, fixed by where their parents/grandparents/ancestors once lived. Identity, however, is not fixed in this way. It is a conjunction of dispositions, experiences, social constructions and so forth; and how someone understands themselves cannot be determined by a conceptual schema, however sophisticated. This is because, though that conceptual schema may be able to suggest that certain forms of life lead to certain choices being made, it cannot provide an adequate description of those factors which influence choices, as these may be indeterminate. In other words, theory is always underdetermined. A particular categorisation system is being used but it could have been a different one, in the sense that it is the type and number of categories within the knowledge domain and the strengths of the boundaries between them which indicate how that domain has been constructed. Since people make judgements on the basis of colour, a naive realist would argue that our category systems must reflect the world as it is. But this is disingenuous because it is through language that we first learn to categorise in the way we do. In short, it is the way language is organised that determines how we actually see that world. In the field of race and ethnicity it is more complicated still, because the category of ethnicity is used as a surrogate for colour. Since it is not acceptable to differentiate on the basis of the colour of someone's skin and since ethnic background constitutes a rough equivalence, it is more acceptable to use the latter rather than the former. If this argument is correct, then category systems are acts of imposition and do not reflect in a straightforward way the nature of reality. The differentiating schema itself is an epistemological construction.

What can this example tell us about whether the middle phase of Weber's schema is value-free or value-relevant? If we choose to identify race as a variable, then we are also choosing (and thus incorporating a value dimension into deliberation) to construct the world in a certain way. What is seemingly a neutral act (the identification of the variable) turns out to be far from neutral. What is frequently neglected from conventional accounts of the research process and, indeed, from Weber's own account is the socially situated nature of the classifications which are central to it. In short, whether researchers like it or not, or even know it or not, they are engaged in making value judgements about what constitutes 'a fact'. Furthermore, this would seem to indicate that Weber's distinction between value-freedom and value-relevance during the second phase of operations is suspect.

Are we then forced to accept the idea that values enter into research at every point and that theory precedes data collection; in short, that 'facts' are determined by theories and that theories are embedded in epistemes or ways of life? Before we accept this conclusion, it is worth examining a number of attempts to refute it. The first is to make a distinction between high-inference and low-inference variables (Phillips, 1993). The example of race alluded to above would be an instance of a high-inference variable and it was suggested that any conceptualisation of this complex idea is shot through at every stage with value assumptions. Indeed, it may be important to try, but ultimately it is not possible to fashion criteria for deciding between different value positions as they relate to race. However, there is a range of low-inference variables of which, as Phillips (1993, p. 63) suggests, 'there is no evidence that people with markedly different theoretical frames – for example, Freudians and behaviourists – actually see different things at the basic or low-level inference level'. However, even here, there are difficulties. The first of these is that, as Harris (1979) suggests, counting the number of people on a university square at a given time is problematic and these problems arise because observers with different belief systems may fail to agree about what a person is. He points to various debates about whether foetuses, newly dead people, vegetated stroke cases and so forth should count as persons. He concludes by arguing that it is not so much that it is impossible to count the number of people in a square, but that in order to do so an observer or group of observers has to agree about definitions, and these definitions are fundamentally belief-orientated. The second problem is more complicated still. How do we actually distinguish between low-level and high-level inference variables, without at the same time falling back on an epistemological or ontological theory?

The second attempt to refute the relativistic implications of theory preceding fact is to argue that built into the research enterprise is a notion of checks and balances. These may comprise more than one observer making the same observation, or more than one data analyst interpreting the same piece of data, or the warranty given by fellow researchers when an article is published in a journal (blind peer review, for example). The first point to note is that consensus-validation may tell us something about the reasonableness of the research activity under scrutiny, but even then it does not enable us to distinguish with any degree of certainty between two oppositely conceived observations or interpretations. The second point is even more disturbing, and this is that this procedure cannot act in any way to refute the claims of relativists; indeed, it actually supports their claims: those claims being that criteria for deciding on knowledge claims and for distinguishing between good and bad research are embedded in locally based communities of knowers who have reached agreement in the past and could do so in the future. However, these do not provide any universal, cross-cultural warrant and, furthermore, they happen as a result of the resolution of power struggles over what constitutes knowledge.

This argument or attempt to provide a justification for objectivity as a useful notion should be distinguished from: 'a view that is objective is one that has been opened up to scrutiny, to vigorous examination, to challenge. It is a view that has been teased out, analysed, criticised, debated – in general, it is a view that has been forced to face the demands of reason and evidence' (Phillips, 1993, p. 65). It is different from the previous argument because it is underpinned by a different epistemological position. In the first argument, consensus is achieved both about what 'a fact' is and, more importantly, about appropriate methods for gathering these 'facts'. In this case, two arguments are being put forward to justify objectivity: that if a conclusion, interpretation or choice of research method is subject to proper examination by other researchers and practitioners, it will benefit from this; and that evidence compels us to accept one interpretation and reject others. Though Phillips has conflated the two, it is important to address the issues separately. The first argument would seem on the surface to be self-evident; however, on closer inspection, the relationship between improvement and peer examination is not as straightforward as it seems. First, it may not necessarily lead to improvement, especially if the power networks which inform such actions are so arranged that what emerges is a compromise. However, it would seem to offer a positive approach to the making of good decisions about research. But even here it cannot lead to any absolute version of knowledge, because the criteria for the activity described above are constructed by communities of knowers which exist at a particular moment in time and space, and are in effect localised.

The second argument may offer us a more secure base for making pronouncements about educational matters. This is that a text is better when it is constructed in terms of the best available evidence. The evidence itself, in the form of data, compels us to draw certain conclusions and it would be wilful to act otherwise. This is regardless, or so the argument goes, of the world-view or positioning of the researcher. This view clearly has some credibility. However, there are certain problems with it. Data are collected in certain specific ways which determine the type of data which are collected, which again determines the type of interpretations that can be made of them. Secondly, it is not at all clear that a piece of data cannot be interpreted in a number of different ways. If we refer back to Gadamer's suggestion that in order to read a text properly (and it is fair to suggest that this also applies to interpreting a data-set or piece of data) one has to place it within a variety of contexts. These contexts may be epistemic, cultural, historical, personal and, even more importantly, methodological. The text has to be read in terms of its pre-texts, sub-texts and inter-texts (Usher, 1997). It is this process which allows us to reflect properly on educational activities. If there is, any longer, mileage in the term objectivity, it is along these lines that we must now proceed. The next chapter presents a view of how educational activities may be structured (the ontological dimension) and the consequences of this for how we may proceed as researchers (the methodological dimension).

3   Educational Knowledge

Ontology

The first of these concerns is ontological. In confronting the sameness of the world, it is possible to suggest that it comprises persistent types of relations between human beings. These relations may be characterised in a number of ways:

- *They persist across time.* Relations between teachers and students, situated in classrooms and schools, though subject to subtle forms of change, have in the main remained the same in different periods of time.
- *They persist across place.* Similar types of relations, for example, between teachers and students, occur in different institutions in the country and indeed round the world. To some extent, this sameness of relations has been accelerated by globalisation and the shortening of time frames between different parts of the world.
- *Social actors in the relational exchange, indeed the many players in the complex game, take on different roles.* Each role is characterised by a set of responsibilities, an accepted way of behaving in that role, expected outcomes and, fundamentally, different amounts of power in relation to other people playing different roles. These relational arrangements may be formalised, in that the rules which underpin the role have been explicitly agreed by the community in various ways and sanctions have been set in place if those rules are broken; or there is an informal agreement about the practising of the role and a degree of negotiation between the different parties about its precise remit and power. The matter is further complicated by the fact that the relative attachment of rewards and sanctions to particular courses of action may change, and with it the degree of risk involved to the person's ontological security.[13]
- *Those relations are characterised by differential amounts of knowledge by the social actors concerned about the actual relations of which they are a part at the precise moment in which those relations are being enacted.*

This is complicated by two factors. The first of these is that the actual form of those relations is partly determined by how they are understood by the social actors concerned. However, it is still possible to differentiate between actual forms of certain relations and how they are understood. This is because it is possible to examine the way social actors come to terms with, or in some cases do not come to terms with, the unexpected difficulty and unexpected degree of sanction they encounter as a result of their fulfilling of the role. Those with a greater degree of knowledge of the contexts in which they operate are likely to have made a better calculation as to which is the best way to meet their ends. The second complication is that since the role itself can never be understood as existing outside of the way it is perceived by the social actor, it is not possible to map precisely the benefits and disbenefits of any course of action proposed by the role holder.

- *These relations are also characterised by the degree of formalisation.* Some behaviours attract sanctions or rewards and are usually inscribed in formal texts. Others have a much looser structure and, though they may attract certain types of sanction or reward, the latter are not formally inscribed or as clearly formulated. Examples of the former type are the awarding of degrees by university charter if the student has completed in a satisfactory manner an explicitly agreed period of study, or the cancelling of an academic's contract of work if they breach certain codes of conduct. An example of the latter is the telling of a joke in a seminar which explicitly discriminates against a minority group.

- *Discursive structures such as gendered and racialised relations which persist at the level of practice may actually occasion sanctions if practised overtly.* They may also operate at the unconscious level, with practitioners, dedicated to their elimination, reproducing such relations because they do not have sufficient knowledge of themselves and relations with other people.

- *Relations are characterised by different knowledge structures.* This includes both how those epistemological constructs are classified and how they are framed. Social actors operate within structures which determine how knowledge is organised and which have differently framed boundaries between the different knowledge constructs.

- Finally, *these relations may be characterised by the degree and type of ownership of material resources.* These allow greater or lesser control over other types of resources in society.

Some of these persistent relations are more resistant to change than others. Whether they change or not depends on: how formalised they are; their perceived usefulness; the fit between this perceived usefulness and other agendas, in particular those held by powerful people in society; the degree and type of organised resistance to them (resistance is a relative term since it depends on the types of control and accountability arrangements made by different nation states in time and place); those sanctions or rewards which are in place; the amount of individual freedom to think and act differently; and the element of chance and the unpredictability of the outcome of human affairs.

Structure and Agency

Given this characterisation of structural properties, we now need to examine the relationship between structure and agency. Though this book is about research and in particular about empirical research, insights from social theory are central to it. Social theory has a long history, and the most intractable problem which it has attempted to solve is the relationship between the individual and society. This has in the last part of the twentieth century been reconceptualised as the relationship between structure and agency, thus incorporating a further element into the dynamic – that of freedom to choose as against being constrained by social forms. Any theory of history which uncovers historical laws and posits a known future is likely to be criticised because it marginalises human agency and indeterminacy. Social forms are identified which work behind the backs of social actors and it is argued that these social forms do not depend on the intentional activity of those self-same human beings. These social forces may comprise class relations, linguistic structures, biological mechanisms or whatever. They all have the effect of reducing the human actor to a position of impotency and have been criticised for reifying institutional properties of society. These can be contrasted with social theories which in turn place an undue emphasis on the creative or intentional dimension of human activity and which as a result downplay the effects of structures, in particular the way human beings are both immersed in and constrained by the way society is constructed.

Archer (1988) has coined a number of terms to identify these and other positions. For her, *downward conflation* refers to the first of our positions, where 'structure and agency are conflated because action is treated as fundamentally epiphenomenal' (Archer, 1990, p. 81), and thus agency is unsuccessfully incorporated into social theory, or to put it another way, neglected. Archer's second position involves what she calls *upward conflation*, and this is where, representing the exact opposite, 'structure is held to be the creation of agency' (ibid., p. 84). She goes on to suggest, for example, that 'the neo-phenomenological school asserts the primacy of agency by reducing the structural context of action to a series of inter-subjectively negotiated constructs' (ibid., p. 84). For her, both these positions are illegitimate. She does, however, suggest two further positions: the first of these is what she calls *central conflation*, popularised by Giddens

(1984) as a theory of structuration; the second is a morphogenetic/ morphostatic framework, which has the virtue for her of avoiding some of the problems implicit in upward, downward and central conflation.

For the time being we need to assert that rejecting both over-socialised and over-individualised perspectives is central to any proper development of social theory and furthermore to the adoption of a coherent methodological stance. The procedures and methods of educational research cannot afford to ignore these insights and therefore have to take account of a properly argued view of both agency and structure and the relationship between them. This position then, immediately distances itself from more pragmatic versions of educational and social research programmes propounded by Bryman (1988)[14] amongst others. How we understand this important relationship is a crucial determining factor in the methods and procedures we adopt as we seek to understand educational practices. An over-socialised view of the relationship condemns us to the adoption of methods which fail to capture the intentional dimension of human agency in the production and reproduction of social institutions. Likewise, too great an emphasis on agency may be reflected in the adoption of methods which signally fail to capture the institutionalised nature of social life.

The most potent of the theories which Archer calls central conflation then is structuration theory. For Giddens (1984, p. 2): 'The basic domain of study of the social sciences, according to the theory of structuration, is neither the experience of the individual actor, nor the existence of any form of social totality, but social practices ordered across space and time.' However, in his desire not to reify these social practices, he is at pains to reconfirm his essential thesis: structural properties exist, and then only fleetingly, in their insubstantiation by social actors as they carry on their daily routinised activities. Structural properties therefore have a virtual existence which again has implications for how they can be known. Though Giddens is prepared to accept that human agents may have acquired a store of tacit knowledge which they are unable to articulate in the course of an interview, for example, and that they may be unaware of many of the structural features which define the contexts within which they act, and even that they may be motivated by unconscious forces which are at odds with their professed reasons for action, '. . . *all social actors, no matter how lowly, have some degree of penetration of the social forms which oppress them*' (ibid., p. 9, my italics). Structural properties therefore cannot be understood or analysed outside of the reasons social actors have for their actions. Furthermore, he argues that:

It is an essential emphasis of the ideas developed here that institutions do not just work 'behind the backs' of the social actors who produce and reproduce them. Every competent member of every society knows a great deal about the institutions of that society: such knowledge is not incidental to the operation of society, but is necessarily involved in it. A common tendency of many otherwise divergent schools of socio-logical thought is to adopt the methodological tactic of beginning their analyses by discounting agents' reasons for their actions (or what I prefer to call the rationalisation of action), in order to discover the 'real' stimuli to their activity, of which they are ignorant. Such a stance is not only defective from the point of view of social theory, it is one with strongly defined and potential offensive political implications. *It implies a derogation of the lay actor.*

(Ibid., p. 8)

This derogation is to be avoided at all costs.

The subject matter of empirical enquiry, its ontology, therefore, avoids any form of reification and at the same time places individuals and collec-tivities of individuals as central to the production and reproduction of social life. For Giddens, the persistent patterning of social life that he and others have observed occurs because of the routinised nature of social life – social actors are much more likely to make choices which reproduce existing structural properties than make choices which lead to limited or funda-mental changes in those structural properties. However, even in this case, the reproductive activity does not go on behind the backs of social actors, but is a consequence of their active participation in the process.

For Archer, one of Giddens' principal critics, structuration theory pro-vides a partial and misguided view of social reproduction and systemic change. She rejects his approach because 'it fails to specify when there will be *more* voluntarism or *more* determinism' (Archer, 1990, p. 77, my italics). She argues that structuration theory embraces two images, both of which she wants to reject: the hyperactivity of agency and 'the rigid coherence of structural properties associated with the essential recursiveness of social life' (ibid.). The first of these follows from Giddens' desire to avoid reifica-tion of structural properties, in that structures are deemed to have only a virtual existence. Thus rules and resources only have substance in their instantiation by human agents. Even in relation to the essentially recursive nature of society, this is only achieved through the active collaboration of agents and groups of agents. Though Giddens denies that he is offering an idealist perspective, the realism of his viewpoint rests on the notion that human beings are actively engaged in the continual process of making and remaking society. It does not rest on the existence of mechanisms in society which may or may not be activated by human agency.

Archer's second charge is that 'Giddens commits himself to an enormous coherence of the structural properties, such that actors' inescapable use of them embroils everyone in the stable reproduction of social systems' (ibid.). The key to Archer's critique is that Giddens' tight binding of struc-ture and agency to avoid structural reification does not allow a judgement to be made about particular structures working on human beings in particular ways, ie. some are more binding than others, and some act in a more coercive way, and that at different time points they may act coercively in different ways and to different degrees. Indeed, depending on circumstances and context, they may not coerce at all. Conversely, the degree of enablement in structural properties can only be determined by empirical investigation of particular activities embedded in particular contexts. As soon as we attempt to specify what that degree of coercion or enablement might be in the form of a theoretical model, we are immediately engaged in a process of reification which as a result fails adequately to describe what actually happened. Archer (1990, p. 78, my italics) therefore argues that:

> . . . action is not so tightly integrated by these structural properties. Not only may some of the smallest items of behaviour be irrelevant to the social system, but certain larger ones may also be trivial, mutually cancelling or self-contained in their effects, while still other actions can produce far-reaching aggregate and emergent consequences. Yet these different possibilities remain undifferentiated by Giddens. What is wrong with this image . . . is that it does not allow for some behaviour engendering replication while other action initiates transformation. Rather than transcending the voluntarism/determinism dichotomy, the two sides of the 'duality of structure' embody them respectively. *They are simply clamped together in a conceptual vice.*

Whether, as Outhwaite (1990) argues, Archer reverts back to a position which effectively reifies structural properties, or whether she succeeds in introducing a flexibility into the relationship between structure and agency which structuration theory is incapable of sustaining, is difficult to determine. Certainly the element of time is crucial to an understanding of social theory and social change, both at the ontological and the epistemological levels.

Structural Properties

If we accept that structural properties exist (and this is a realist assumption),[15] and that they have capacities to influence action (by virtue of having attached to them sanctions or rewards), then we need to identify two forms of relations. The first is those capacities, which may or may not be exercised, and the second is how they are exercised, if they are exercised at all. These structural properties may refer to discourses which have no material existence, or to discourses embedded in texts, or formalised in laws, or to institutional arrangements. As we suggested above, each of these types of structural property have different degrees of sanction or enablement attached to them. Thus a patriarchal discourse may be challenged or resisted at the systems level, ie. by equal opportunities legislation, or at the interactional level, ie. by the transformation of married relations (not the institutional aspects of marriage but the day-to-day activities which constitute marriage). The discourse itself, which is real in that it operates outside of any reproducing or transforming activity by individual social actors or groups of social actors, can only be understood by how it influences action. The structure therefore may be described as having strong or weak powers, or degrees of both. There reaches a point when its powers become so weak that the discursive formation can no longer be thought of as relevant to any study of social life as it is. What essentially has changed is that the sanctions and enablements attached to it are no longer considered strong enough to affect human behaviour and more importantly human relations. When this happens, it is possible to talk about a new discursive formation by virtue of the new discourse having powers to influence human relations and it has those powers by virtue of its ability to attach rewards and sanctions to particular types of behaviour.

Discourses or traditions of thought therefore are manifested in real human behaviour, are subject to change and decay, may be hierarchically organised and more importantly are nested within supra-discourses.[16] These latter discourses operate at the epistemological and ontological levels; that is, the way a society or group of people understands the nature of the world and how it can be known influences the types of ordinary discourses which operate within that society. Furthermore, they influence the rate of decay of those discourses.

We now need to turn our attention to other types of structure which are manifested in formal roles, and which combine in various ways to form institutions (in the case we are examining in this book, they will be families, schools, colleges and universities) and systems (whose function is to coordinate those primary institutions). These roles have attached to them potential powers; that is capacities to influence relations between human beings and groups of human beings. Again, they work by allocating rewards and sanctions to activities they deem to be their focus.

We could take as an example a head teacher in a school. Head teachers operate within hierarchical structures which pre-exist any one person's assumption of the role. Thus the role has powers and possibilities which attach to the role and not to the person. However, different head teachers may play out that role in different ways. The first scenario is where head teachers have knowledge of the structural properties of their role (never perfect but sufficient) and they exploit them to their fullest degree, and in the process reproduce the structural properties of their role, though never perfectly. The second scenario is where they have knowledge of those structures (never perfect but sufficient) and they then seek to transform them by undermining those hierarchical relations which pre-existed their assumption of the role. This has certain dangers because changes to hierarchical relations in one part of the system have consequences for other parts and indeed depend for their existence on how other parts are organised; in other words, in doing so, they transform the roles of others. However, because they are acting in isolation, there is no guarantee that any change will occur at the systems level or indeed that the powers and liabilities of that role per se have changed. On the other hand, if enough head teachers behaved like this, then systems level transformation may take place. The important point to note is that the structural property in this case (when the assumption is made of sufficient knowledgeability) has influenced the agency of a particular head teacher, whether by seeking to change the status quo (the change is a reaction against what was) or reproducing it. However, as we suggested, whether that structural property remains influential is dependent on a large number of other interactions and agential decisions within the system.

The third option allows us to examine the knowledgeability of the social actor whose actions transform or reproduce the existing status quo. Head teachers do not have proper knowledge of these structures (an unlikely scenario anyway). They, in other words, have a distorted view of those structures and believe, for example, that relations within their school are egalitarian and that roles are not hierarchically arranged. As a result, they are likely to operate ineffectually because, as we suggested above, systems of roles are nested in other systems. By undermining the structural properties of a school through ignorance, they are likely to make inadequate judgements about their capacity to achieve the change they want to make – both structural and everyday. However, they have transformed the nature of those structures, even if through ignorance of them, and if enough head teachers behaved in this way and enough teachers or administrators did not impede the transformation in each school, then the structural relations would have been changed, albeit not as intended.

At any one point in time within a system a number of differently organised struggles may be going on. This is because those structural properties do not automatically carry with them benefits and disbenefits which compel role-holders to behave in certain ways. Role-holders may reproduce the role, ie. act in terms of the structural properties of the role; or they may seek to subvert the role by disregarding the balance of benefits and disbenefits the role has attached to it; or more importantly they may either be ignorant of them or understand them in a way that is not prescribed by the role.

Methodology

There are also methodological implications of the framework developed above. Giddens (1984) elucidates four levels of social research. The first is the hermeneutic elucidation of the frame of meaning of the social actor(s) involved. The second is the investigation of context and the form of practical consciousness. The third is the identification of the bounds of knowledgeability and the fourth is the specification of institutional orders. His argument is that quantitative researchers either pay insufficient attention to the first or collect data about it in the wrong order or ignore it altogether. What this schema also implies is that a purely phenomenological perspective is inadequate. This is so for four reasons: first, social actors operate within unacknowledged conditions, that is, societal structures within which the actor is positioned; second, there are unintended consequences of his/her actions; third, social actors operate through tacit knowledge which is hidden by virtue of what it is, or at least is not articulated during the formation of explanations of action; fourth, the social actor may be influenced by unconscious motivation. What this points to is the inevitable objectification involved in social research (that is the going beyond the purely phenomenological perspective) (cf. Bhaskar, 1989). However, as Giddens argues, this going beyond, in order for the explanation to be valid, has to involve an understanding of the perspectives of social actors and the implications of this is that methods have to be used which do not distort those meanings. There is always an ethnographic moment[17] in social research and this cannot legitimately be written out by quantitative researchers.

Educational researchers therefore need to examine the following:

- *Relations or structural properties at each time point* – These may or may not have been activated in the particular circumstances under investigation, but provide access to understanding the essential contexts of action.
- *Interpretations of those relations by relevant social actors* – These need to be collected by researchers because they provide access to those structural properties which position social actors.
- *Relations between different structures at each time point* – Instead of assuming that a structural property always operates to effect human actions and interactions at every time point, it is important to understand when, where and how these different structures are influential; and furthermore, what the precise relationship is between them at specific moments and places during these interactions.
- *Perceived relations between different structures at each time point by the relevant social actors* – This is a necessary part of the research process for two reasons. First, it provides access for the researcher to those real relations referred to above. Second, social actors' perceptions of those relations constitute a part of them.
- *The intentions of social actors in the research setting* – Actors may also be motivated by unconscious forces which compel them to behave in certain ways and which may conflict with the accounts they give of

their reasons for action. By examining the intentions of social actors, it is possible to make a judgement about how much they know and how this impacts on decisions they make.

- *The unintended consequences of actions* – Some activities may be designed, and thus have a degree of intention behind them, which has the effect of changing structural properties; others less so. But, more importantly, all actions have unintended consequences to some degree. This is an important dimension to the research enterprise.
- *The subsequent effects of those intended and unintended actions on structural properties* – After each interaction, however limited, it is important to assess its effects on those structures which provide the contexts for future exchanges and interactions.
- *The degree of structural influence and the degree of agential freedom for each human interaction* – This is the crux of the matter because it allows the researcher to understand the complex relationship between agency and structure at each time point.

The next chapter examines the problems with, and the possibilities of, an influential research strategy in the field of education, mathematical modelling.

4   Mathematical Modelling

This chapter focuses on mathematical modelling in educational research. The fact that, increasingly in this field, the predominance of quantitative methods is evident, may lead one to conclude that the quantitative/ qualitative debate has been settled in favour of the former.[18] To some extent, this is as a result of managerial pressures and the need to produce research findings which allow predictions to be made by managers, at both institutional and systemic levels. In addition, they reflect scientistic pressures to mirror the procedures and methods of the natural sciences: that predictive, determinate, rational and impersonal knowledge is possible in the social sciences and that our failure to solve many of the problems in society reflects a distortion of those methods rather than the application of a misguided epistemology and ontology. However, we need to examine whether in fact the world can be known in this way; whether, in other words, a distortion occurs when educationalists revert to mathematical modelling.

The method is underpinned by a number of beliefs about the nature of reality and how we can know it, which immediately involves us in a contradiction, since one of those assertions is that such methods are not reflections of underlying belief systems. There are two main types of quantitative approach: deterministic modelling and statistical manipulation. Sayer (1992) distinguishes between: 1) experimental controls where the variable is held constant, for example, controlling the pedagogic input into the teaching of literacy via a series of pre-arranged computer programs (though it is doubtful if all the pedagogic input can be accounted for in this way); 2) observational controls where the variable happens to be constant, for example, comparing classes in school which have the same number and types of children; 3) mathematical controls where post-hoc manipulation of the effects of a variable are made even if those effects have not been controlled for in real life.

Deterministic modellers (and these are more likely to comprise experimentalists or observers) reduce aspects of human behaviour to variables which are self-sufficient and logically distinct and all aspects of social life are reduced in this way. Social life consists of a number of instances of those variables which are, for the purposes of description, equivalent, and this equivalence operates across time and place. The relationship between these variables is causal and linear. Furthermore, both material artefacts and human behaviour can be characterised in this way, so that the intentions, beliefs and reasons for action by human beings are no different from the activities of chemicals. Antecedent conditions are understood as efficient causes of human behaviour. This means that it is possible to develop a science of human behaviour which allows predictions to be made about what will happen.

With statistical manipulators however, the system so described is not determinate as such because built into it is a notion of probability which allows for the possibility of counter-factual cases. Even then, we may some-times be wrong about the nature of the world, but this is caused by the bias of the researcher or observer, when they fail to bracket out their values, pre-conceptions and experiences of the world or inappropriately apply the method. Values or preferences or choices do not play a significant part in either the activities of human beings or their description by other human beings. Furthermore, within the limits of probability, it is possible to pro-vide policy-makers, administrators and the like with information which they can then confidently use to further their ends. This argument therefore seems on the surface to have provided us with a solution to our problem, which is finding a means of obtaining useful knowledge but which at the same time is able to account for a voluntaristic dimension to human relations.

Systematic Unpredictability

However, this may present too simple a view of explanation in the social sciences. Macintyre (1981) argues that there are four sources of systematic unpredictability. There is the possibility of radical conceptual innovation: 'any invention, any discovery, which consists essentially in the elaboration of a radically new concept cannot be predicted, for a necessary part of the prediction is the present elaboration of the very concept whose discovery or invention was to take place only in the future' (ibid., p. 89). This could be explained after the event and is therefore in theory explicable, but could not be predictable or at least the explanation could not involve what is going to happen. Second, there is the impossibility of both the observer and the observed being able to predict what they will do and what the other will do, because in being confronted by a number of alternative choices, they have not yet made the choice confronting them and therefore cannot predict what that choice will be. If the person was all-knowing and was therefore able to predict what choice they would make, they would not then have to or be in a position to make it, because it would have already been determined. Since they are not all-knowing, it is impossible for them to predict what they will do. Third, because game players in any situation reflexively monitor their situation and thus change their stance in relation to how they perceive what is going on and because they also seek to prevent their behaviour from being seen as predictable, this has two implications. It is not possible to predict – that is say what they will do in the future – because that reflexive monitoring has the potential to change the conditions in which they are acting and thus render future actions unpredictable. Furthermore, because the game itself or its rules may change, including the substitution of some players for others and, potentially more important, new distributions of power between players, it is not possible to understand the situation as determinate. As Macintyre (1981, p. 94) puts it: 'There is at the outset no determinate, enumerable set of factors, the totality of which comprise the situation. To suppose otherwise is to confuse a retrospective standpoint with a prospective one.' The fourth of Macintyre's sources of unpredictability in human affairs is what he calls pure contingency. Though mathematical modellers claim to be able to determine the chance factor inherent in any relationship between variables and thus eliminate it from their explanation, any explanation of what actually happened, for it to be a complete one, has to embrace the notion of chance, for it is chance that provides the most sensible explanation.

For Macintyre, these provide obstacles to the development of a science of human behaviour. In essence, he is resisting a determinate view of human nature, because he is suggesting both that human affairs are to some extent indeterminate and therefore unpredictable, and that the observer operates from the same perspective. The sensible course of action for him or her is to act retrospectively rather than prospectively. And yet, as we suggested above, there is a possible solution to this dilemma for mathematical modellers. This is that because human life is essentially routinised and consists of the constant conjunction of events or activities, it is possible to understand what will happen in the future in probabilistic terms. This allows for the possibility of counter-factual cases where the individuals involved have not behaved as they should, or to put it in another way, have behaved in an unpredictable way. However, this attempted solution attempts to map at the systems level and not at the individual level. It is therefore inevitably not concerned with individual reflexive action or with the fate of individuals. Furthermore, because it operates at the structural level, it assumes that those structures will remain intact between T_1 – the present – and T_2 – the future. Structures are human creations; they are only sustained in their present form through a series of similar actions of other human beings in the past; and they only undergo change in their basic structure because sufficient numbers of human beings resist those self-same impulses and in effect create something anew. Furthermore, there is a sense in which those probabilities are merely a reflection of our relative ignorance about the precise causal relations which concern us. As we learn more about *a* causing *b* to happen, we are less concerned with expressing the relationship as a probable one. Expressing the future in probabilistic terms does not solve the problem of the indeterminacy of human relations. It merely identifies the proportion of counter-factual cases which are likely to occur, and this again operates proportionately in relation to the relative degree of development of the theory which is being espoused. Indeed, if we had perfect knowledge of events and their causes we would not have to express them in probabilistic terms at all; but even then, we would only have knowledge of past events and would not be entitled to make prospective judgements.

Furthermore, we have the problem of what Giddens (1984) calls 'the double hermeneutic', which, though he accepts may allow structures and routines of social life to remain relatively stable, always has the potentiality for instability.[19] This is because any descriptions we make of social life, especially if formalised in influential texts, have the effect of adding to the sum of knowledge about human affairs and changing it – in effect knowledge undermines itself when disseminated. This is because knowledge is public and thus has the potentiality to be resisted or incorporated into discourses in ways which are not predictable, and this therefore has the effect of changing that self-same reality and rendering the original explanation invalid.

These are powerful arguments against mathematical modelling, whether of a deterministic or probabilistic kind. There are three additional arguments which need to be examined: 1) educational and social researchers operate within open systems of social relations and as a result change over time can only be understood qualitatively; 2) if we make the assumption that the world consists of constant conjunctions of events, this inevitably conflates associations and causal relations. On the other hand, if we adopt a generative rather than successionist view of causation, this allows us to incorporate an indeterminate dimension to the way we understand the world;[20] 3) the reduction involved in quantitative modelling acts to trivialise and/or distort social relations (this operates at the epistemological level). As a result of this reduction, the intensional dimension of social life is neglected with a consequent damage done to the veracity of the explanations we produce.

Closed and Open Systems

The first of these propositions is that a distinction needs to be made between closed and open systems.[21] Closed systems operate in two ways. First, they operate consistently: that is, there must be no change in the object which is the repository of those causal powers we are interested in between different cases; and this refers to all the possible cases, now and in the future. Second, the external conditions of the causal mechanism must remain constant to allow it to operate. Thus it is possible to suggest that when both these conditions hold, we can infer a causal relation, in which regularities are produced. There is of course a third condition which lies in the realm of epistemology, and this is that the knowing of this causal relationship has not been contaminated by faulty, inconsistent or inadequate methods of data collection.

We have referred here to the realist notion of a mechanism. By this is meant that an object has powers and capabilities which are causally efficacious. Something results in the world as a direct and necessary consequence of the activation of these powers and liabilities. Furthermore, those powers and liabilities do not just reside in individual human beings but also in the relations between them and indeed in the structural forms which they reproduce and change by their voluntaristic actions. Since human beings are both individual and immersed in, indeed creators of, societies, causal powers can operate at both levels. They do not, however, operate in any deterministic way and are only activated by individuals and groups of individuals creating the conditions for them to do so. In other words, they may lie dormant and not be actualised. This is because human relations take place in open systems. Here, the two conditions which pertain to closed systems are violated. Objects do not operate consistently. That is, they change their essential nature, so that it is difficult to argue that there is no change in the object we are interested in between different cases. More commonly, the external conditions for the exercise of those causal mechanisms change also, thus again it is likely that over time and in different places different and non-equivalent manifestations of those causal powers at work are in operation. There is of course a third possibility, which is that the intrinsic condition of closure remains the same, ie. is relatively enduring, but the conditions for its realisation do not remain constant.

The natural sciences in general operate with closed systems[22] and indeed natural scientists may deliberately create conditions which mirror them, ie. working in controlled laboratory conditions, where they seek in particular to control those external conditions which may contaminate the workings of the system. The social sciences have in general a more difficult task: first, because the objects with which they are dealing – individual behaviour, relations between individuals and structural properties of systems – are more likely to change across time and be different in different settings, and because those external conditions which allow those powers and capabilities to be manifested do not remain constant.

An example in the field of education comprises the differential achievements of boys and girls at school. Fifteen years ago in the United Kingdom, boys were outperforming girls in the majority of school subjects (T_1). The situation, though not reversed, has changed radically, with girls now outperforming boys in most if not all subjects at every level of the system (T_2).[23] What has changed? First, the object itself, the boy or girl (the person expressed exclusively in gendered terms) has changed. It is possible to identify the nature of some of these changes, ie. the degree of confidence expressed as varying qualities of being male or female; the type of identity they have as a gendered being; how they understand themselves as male or female in a gendered world and so on. In short, the object has not remained stable, or at least we cannot make the assumption that the gendered nature of the object over time has remained the same. Indeed, we would expect it to be different. However, by virtue of the fact that the object has changed its identity over time, the first condition for the operation of a closed system has been violated.

Furthermore, it is possible to suggest that the external conditions for closed systems in this case have in like fashion not proved constant. The mechanism which involves learning and hence the performance of girls and boys has also changed. Again, we can posit the notion that the learning conditions and experiences of boys and girls in schools and elsewhere has been transformed by the active concern of teachers who have in the past discriminated, albeit unconsciously, against girls. They have, for all sorts of reasons, changed their approach to teaching and learning. Furthermore, socio-economic conditions, such as the availability of certain types of jobs in the labour market, have changed, which has in turn changed the equation with regards to the worthwhileness of studying at school for boys and girls. As Sayer (1992, p. 177) argues: 'assumptions of linearity, additivity and of the possibility of discovering practically adequate instrumentalist laws of proportional variation all depend for their success on a particular material property of the objects to which they refer'. Mathematical modelling of objects that change across time is only possible if the type of change involved is either purely quantitative or 'reducible to the movement of qualitatively unchanging entities' (ibid., p. 177). If that change is irreducibly qualitative, then like is not being compared with like and the mathematical operations referred to above are not appropriate. In our example both the object itself and the conditions for its realisation are subject to qualitative change (even if similar words are being used to describe the two situations at T_1 and T_2).

The situation is further complicated, as we suggested above, by the place and role of the researcher in the equation. It is interesting that the reversal in relative performance between girls and boys has occurred so rapidly, given the stubborn resistance to change exhibited by institutional and relational arrangements. This may be to do with the measuring devices used. There is some evidence to suggest that changes to the examination technology have favoured girls at the expense of boys or at least redressed the balance (Gipps and Murphy, 1994). (No device is going to produce perfect equity because all examination devices are culturally located, but given the existing conditions for performance in examinations, it is suggested that a form of gender bias has been redressed with the consequence that boys are relatively disadvantaged and girls relatively advantaged compared with what they were before.)

The point being made here is that our explanation has involved violation of a number of the principles which are central to our model of a closed system. Indeed, educational researchers are clearly operating within open systems. There are a number of implications. First, the constant conjunction of events that we think we have observed is not what it seems. Second, the construction of a mathematical model allows us to (with the limitations expressed above) establish a differential relation between the two variables – gender and performance – but it does not allow us to describe a causal relationship. In order to do this, we would need to examine qualitatively the various ways the mechanism works or does not work, because the conditions for it to work may or may not be operating. If it is argued, as Goldstein and Myers (1997) do, that it is possible to plot the different ways those relations have changed, both in terms of the object and the conditions for its manifestation, then certainly we can do this, but we cannot do it using the methods appropriate to closed systems. In other words, the principle of equivalence is central to the application of such mathematical methods and we can either ignore this particular issue or accept that the non-equivalence of objects and conditions over a period of time calls for different methods. Finally, it is important to understand that the methods or techniques of data collection themselves are subject to cultural and therefore socio-historical contextualisation.

Association and Causation

The second problem is the precise relationship between association and causation. Associations are identified as being between precisely defined variables. These variables have to be operationalised and this means that they have to be understood and expressed as observable phenomena. Furthermore, they cannot be singular because the defining operation of which they are a part involves the further identification of other identifiable items which are similar in all essential respects. There is in addition a necessary reductive act involved in the process of operationalising the variable, and one moreover which denies the need for any interpretive activity. By reductive process is meant the operation of placing a particular act or action within a group of like acts or actions.

If we take as an example a boy living in a large city whose parents have a low (in relative terms) combined income, we may want to understand why his results at GCSE are relatively poor. The argument is as follows and it is indeed complicated. A general probabilistic association has been established between children's achievements at school and relative levels of poverty experienced by those children. In the first place the reduction which has been made is to two groups – a relatively rich one (A) and a relatively poor one (B). A simple process of arithmetic will suffice. If all the examination results of group A are added together, they can be shown to have exceeded the combined results of all the children in group B. If we now want to make the argument more sophisticated, we may want to construe our syllogism as: the more poor the family is, the less likely the children are to do well in GCSE examinations. The reduction has become more refined, because children are now being assigned to a number of groups, as indeed are their results at GCSE. However, the larger the number of groups in each column the less likely they will perfectly correlate with each other. We could have created one-person groups and the correlation is now likely to be far from perfect. In other words, as soon as we do this we are identifying counter-factual cases, and the less we have to rely on probabilities. If we ever choose to assign children to groups using pre-specified criteria, we have to build in a probability factor. The point being made here is that the greater the reduction of a characteristic, the more we have to rely on a probability factor; and the more refinement in our reduction, the less reliance there is on a probability factor and therefore the less likelihood that there will be an error in any prediction we make about an individual child.

The next problem we have to solve is how we operationalise each of our two variables and what degree of reduction we think is acceptable (we have already suggested that reduction and probability work in an inverse proportional way). The first of our variables is poverty, and in order to determine which children are relatively poor and which children are relatively rich, we have to devise an indicator which can be operationalised. What this means is that as researchers we have to be in a position to collect data about it which is both reliable and valid; that is it operates across all the cases in the same way and actually refers to what we want it to refer to. Now both of these are problematic. We could collect data by asking the parents of our sample what their income is. However, they may refuse to give us that information or indeed if they do, they may, for all sorts of good reasons, give us false information. If we do succeed in collecting this information we may have to make a calculation about its reliability. Now we can do this in a number of ways – the most widely used would be to compare it with another set of data which purported to refer to the same characteristic, ie. poverty. This could be take-up of free school meals by the parents or the area in which the family live (perhaps measured by house prices) and so forth.

Let us look at these two measures in detail, with the understanding that these are only two examples of proxy measures for determining the relative poverty of a family. In the first case, as we have already suggested, because the reduction of our sample is relatively crude, ie. between those who are receiving free school meals and those who are not, the greater the need there is to understand the association which we are trying to establish as probabilistic – in other words, there are bound to be more counter-factual cases. Furthermore, the other problem which we identified above, that of the reliability of the data, presents practical problems. Since parents can claim free school meals for their children if they declare that their joint income is below a certain level, this measure relies on parents making an honest assessment of their incomes. Such a self assessment is open to fraudulent behaviour and/or unintentional misrepresentation. In our second example of a proxy measure – house prices – again this may not provide us with a particularly accurate account of poverty for a number of reasons. Families may have bought their house when they were relatively poor and became attached to it, even if they have now accumulated a reasonable amount of money and would be classified as relatively rich. They may have another house elsewhere which is not taken into consideration. Furthermore, we know that house prices are determined by a host of other factors which do not reflect the income or level of poverty of the family. For instance, a local school manages to turn itself from a failing to a successful and therefore popular school. This attracts a new income-related type of family to the area which is likely to raise the house prices within that area, even if the income of many of the original families who stayed has not changed.

However, there is a more serious problem, and this relates to our original specification of the association which we are trying to understand. Poverty itself is a proxy measure of something else, in the same way as achievement at GCSE represents something else, ie. learning (however this is defined and/or understood). Poverty in its own right does not cause poor examination results. What does may be in a probable association with relative levels of poverty. There are a number of possibilities: families which are poor have less space to live in and therefore children may find it harder to complete their homework which in turn may mean that they learn less well, which again may mean that they perform less well in examinations. Or, families which are poor have poorer diets and this has an effect on the ability of the child to concentrate which means that they learn less quickly and therefore perform less well in examinations. Or, as Bourdieu and Passeron (1980) have suggested, poorer families have less cultural capital, which means that their ability to access pedagogical interactions is limited, which in turn may mean that in conventional terms they learn less and therefore do less well in examinations. Or, to paraphrase a familiar explanation, their parents place less emphasis on the process of schooling, either because they do not understand its import or because they genuinely do not believe that it can contribute to the future lifestyles of their children, which again means that the child does not try as hard as they could at school, which again means that they perform less well in examinations.

I have laboured the point, but it is still worth making. The measures which are usually used to determine the relationship between poverty and achievement in school are approximations or proxies to the real variables which are implicated in the causal mechanism which may or may not be operationalised. However, it is more complicated still, because the possible causal mechanisms which we identified above may be relevant to some children and not to others, even if all these children are relatively poor. Furthermore, a causal mechanism may operate for a particular child at a particular point in their life, but then be replaced by another later. And which mechanism operates at which point in time depends as much on the individual child and on the environments in which they live and work as on anything else. The variable that is used is almost bound to be a proxy measure, and this means that it may impoverish the description of the relevant causal mechanism. In part, this is because of the reductive process which mathematical modellers use. The relationship therefore between, for example, poverty and reading problems[24] is associational and may tell us little about the causal mechanism which produces the association. And this is in part because mathematical modellers have assumed a successionist rather than a generative theory of causation. Indeed, as Bhaskar (1979) suggests, in his discussion of transcendental realism, those regularities so produced do not relate in a straightforward way to the causal mechanism which produced them. Indeed, those deeper-lying structures or causal mechanisms may actually contradict or be in conflict with their appearances. Those theorists who operate in closed systems do not have to cope with this problem; those who operate in open systems, however, have to distinguish between associational properties and causal mechanisms.

We also need to examine the other variable – examination performance – and to try to understand that this is also a proxy measure. Mathematical modelling of schooling measures performance in a standardised way – to allow comparisons between individual pupils in different settings. Furthermore, modellers choose those attributes which can be more easily quantified (ie. reading ages as they are measured on a standardised test) or which have already been quantified (ie. GCSE, Key Stage Tests or 'A' level scores). Performance is emphasised and this is performance of a kind which can be reliably quantified. However, these measurements refer to performance at a certain point in time and in controlled conditions and not to the levels of competence reached by the child. Wood and Power (1987) distinguish between performance and competence (see Table 4.1) and develop this distinction along two axes. The first relates to performance in the test situation – whether the child is successful or unsuccessful at the task. The second axis refers to what the child can do. Thus two types of errors may result – false negative and false positive – and these occur because of the gap between competence and performance. However, it is impossible to separate these two in any meaningful way. This is so for two reasons: first, the levels of

Table 4.1 Error types in relating performance to competence

	Success on Task	*Failure on Task*
Child has underlying competence (in sufficient degree)	Performance correlated with competence	False negative error: failure due to factor other than lack of competence
Child does not have underlying competence (in sufficient degree)	False positive error: success due to factor other than competence	Performance correlated with competence

Source: Wood and Power (1987)

performance achieved by children influence what and how they learn and therefore affect the competence levels they achieve at a later point in time; second, the gap between competence and performance for individual children varies and cannot be measured. If it is suggested that a more accurate expression of competence could be obtained by repeated testing and repeated measurement, this cannot solve the problem, since for some children it is those factors which inhere in the testing process itself which sustain the gap between performance and competence. False negative errors in testing make reference to an ideal which can be inferred but not quantified. If it could then it would be possible to argue that, with a more sophisticated testing technology, the gap between competence and performance could be eliminated. Researchers could then be certain that a child's performance accurately reflects what he or she is able to do. Hammersley (1992) distinguishes between different meanings of the word 'accuracy' when he argues that precision or accuracy may not be best expressed quantitatively. Accurate descriptions of phenomena depend on their relation to the objects to which they refer and not to their ability to be expressed in mathematical form.

It is possible to go beyond this and suggest that the distinction between competence and performance referred to above implies a particular way of understanding this relationship and is therefore a theory-laden concept. Vygotsky (1978) argues that a more useful notion of performance does not refer to the ability of the child to operate in standardised conditions but to the ability of that child to perform in conditions which maximise performance, and this of course might include collaboration between child and adult/teacher/tester. This refers to the zone of proximal development: competence is here being defined as the capability of the child to progress to higher levels of learning. It therefore cannot be measured for a number of reasons: best, rather than typical, performances are examined; it takes place in relatively uncontrolled conditions; it is essentially ipsative and thus seeks to make comparisons between different performances of the child rather than between performances of different children (cf. Gipps,

1994). This would suggest that standardised approaches to the collection of data used by mathematical modellers imply a theory about assessment and do not simply measure what is.

A second problem with using test scores is different. This is to do with the reliability of the marking of such tests. Nuttall (1995, p. 57) reminds us that 'research evidence suggests that the margin of error in a candidate's grade at 'O' level or CSE is about one grade in every direction'. Again it can be argued that if researchers compare school with school, each school has the same chance of marking error with regard to their scores and that therefore the comparison is still valid. However if multi-level modelling techniques are used as in many school effectiveness research projects (cf. Goldstein, 1987) with their reliance on data gathered at the individual level and matched pairs of children, this matching becomes suspect.[25]

Intensionality and Extensionality

We now come to the third of our arguments against mathematical modelling. This is that, because modellers operate extensionally, the intensional dimension of social life is neglected. Behaviourism, for example, located within a natural science model of explanation, seeks to eliminate any references to beliefs, purpose and meaning. However, a social science or hermeneutic science of human behaviour would embrace these human traits and suggest that social actors' descriptions of their experiences, projects and desires are not purely epiphenomenal. If they are treated as such, then this acts to reify social relations. This reification means that social relations and the constant conjunction of their manifestations are explained without reference to the way they are understood and described by social actors. However, if we reject this, it is important that we do not then conclude that social actors have a complete and accurate picture of what is going on, even though we can and must allow these self-descriptions to be essential components of the way we understand social life. (Reference to this has already been made in the previous chapter.)

What follows from this? First, as Wilson (1990, pp. 398–399) argues:

> It is crucially important to note explicitly that use of a mathematical model does not imply that descriptions are untainted by intension. Rather, when we develop and apply such a model we arrange to package intensional idioms in such a way that, for the purposes at hand, we can proceed with formal calculations.

Because variables have to be able to be expressed quantitatively, they have to adhere to the principle of equivalence. The category system which is used, for example racial classification, has to ignore the many complications that inhere in the production of such lists, not least that the social actors concerned may refuse to accept the criteria which underpin the category system or may be coerced into accepting it (as in the census). Thus, for the sake of the modelling exercise, the intensional idiom, and it is this after all which is central to our understanding of the issue, is reduced or packaged so that it can be expressed as an extensional property.

The second implication is more serious still. It is that these social actors and the relations between them are reduced to pale shadows of their real selves. Structural properties are reified and the voluntaristic dimension to social life is inadequately accounted for. The arguments suggested in this chapter, against mathematical modelling, need to be taken seriously if we are ever to properly understand social life and educational activities. An example of mathematical modelling and its attendant problems is given in Chapter 6. Meanwhile, the issue of how we can conceptualise the theory–practice relationship is addressed in the next chapter.

5 Theory into Practice

Five Versions

For those concerned to provide accounts of educational practice, conceptualising the relationship between the theory they produce and the practice which they are describing is central to their activities. In short, how this relationship is understood is important both because it affects the type of account produced and because it impacts upon the improvement of practices per se. There are five possible positions which can be taken, with proponents of each adopting different viewpoints as to how theory about educational practices is constructed and how it relates to those self-same educational practices.

The first of these is what Habermas calls scientistic.[26] This means, for him, 'science's belief in itself: that is, the conviction that we can no longer understand science as *one* form of possible knowledge, but rather must identify knowledge *with* science' (Habermas, 1974, p. 4). There is a correct method for collecting data about educational activities. This method, if properly adhered to, leads to the creation of objective, value-free and authoritative knowledge about how educators should behave. Practitioners therefore need to 'bracket out' their own values, experiences and preconceptions because these are partial, incomplete and subjective and follow the precepts of researchers whose sole purpose is to develop knowledge which transcends the local and the contextual.

Scientific theory is designated as theory because relations between educational phenomena are being expressed at a general level; that is, they apply to a variety of situations both in the present and in the future. It therefore allows prediction, not, it should be noted, because the expression of that theory influences what will happen but because the knowledge itself is propositional, generalisable, non-particularistic and operates outside the realm of actual practice. The criteria which determine good practice in scientific research comprise in part a particular relationship to practitioner knowledge: that the former is superior to the latter, and that appropriate behaviour on the part of the practitioner would consist of correcting and amending errors to their own knowledge domain in the light of what is being asserted as a result of the correct scientific procedures being followed. Practice is conceived of as the following of rules which have been systematically researched and formalised as theory.[27] This has been described as the technical-rationality model of the theory–practice relationship in which practice is understood as the practical application of a body of theoretical knowledge. Worthwhile knowledge is understood as being located in the field of generalised propositions; practice is not conceived of as knowledge at all but as the application of theory in practical situations.

Proponents of this view make a number of assumptions: first and foremost, that theoretical knowledge can give us insights into reality; that is, it can provide adequate and meaningful descriptions of how the world works. It therefore assumes a naive realist perspective and one which denigrates actors' perceptions of how the world works because these may be partial, inaccurate, ideologically motivated or falsely conceived. Second, practice itself or practical knowledge is not in itself sufficiently robust to qualify as knowledge, ie. the criteria we apply for something to qualify as knowledge (for example, consistency, coherence, validity, reliability and generalisability) cannot be applied to practical deliberation. Schon (1983) argues that this conception of the theory–practice dynamic cannot itself provide an adequate description of the relationship. Furthermore, this privileging of theoretical knowledge over practical knowledge has to be understood as a consequence of history and not as an a priori theoretical truth.

The second perspective has some similarities to the scientistic viewpoint, but understands the creation of objectified knowledge in a different way. Proponents of this viewpoint would want to adopt a realist perspective but would understand that realist perspective in a different way – they might want to adopt a generative rather than successionist theory of causal relations or they might want to reconceptualise the researcher–researched relationship so that the value perspectives of the researcher are centrally implicated in the act of doing research.[28] However, the educational text that is produced is still treated in the same way as with our first perspective and the relationship between theory and practice is understood as being consistent with the technical-rationality model referred to above. Usher et al. (1996, p. 26) describe this model as:

> . . . the solving of technical problems through rational decision-making based on predictive knowledge. It is the means to achieve ends where the assumption is that ends to which practice is directed can always be predefined and are always knowable. The condition of practice is the learning of a body of theoretical knowledge, and practice therefore becomes the application of this body of knowledge in repeated and predictable ways to achieve predefined ends.

Both of our first two perspectives, therefore, different though they are, are concerned with determining a measure of technical efficiency which will per se lead to the achievement of ends which are separate from the determination of means regarded as necessary to their realisation.

The third type of theory–practice relationship is multi-perspectival and multi-methodological. If there is no correct method, but only a set of methods which produce texts of various kinds and these can be read in different ways, then the practitioner has to make a series of decisions about which text is appropriate and which is not. Theory and practice are here being uncoupled. Whether or not the practitioner works to the prescriptive framework of the theorist will depend on a number of factors, such as the fit between the values of the theorist and the practitioner, whether they share a common epistemological framework, and, fundamentally, whether solutions are being provided by the theorist to practical problems encountered during the practitioner's everyday activity. The practitioner is here being treated as a self-sufficient producer and user of knowledge. However, there is still a sense with this perspective that the outside theorist can produce broadly accurate prescriptive knowledge which because of the contingencies of life in educational institutions then needs to be adapted to the settings in which the practitioner works. The theorist produces general knowledge, the practitioner supplies the fine-grained detail, but in all essential respects still follows precepts developed by outside theorists.

A fourth position which can be taken is an extension of the logic expressed above. Walsh (1993, p. 43) describes it as an interpretation of the theory–practice relationship which 'turns on the perception that deliberated, thoughtful practice is not just the target, but is the major source (perhaps the specifying source) of educational theory'. Furthermore, he suggests that 'there is now a growing confidence within these new fields that their kind of theorizing, relating closely and dialectically with practice, is actually the core of educational studies and not just the endpoint of a system for adopting and delivering outside theories' (ibid., p. 43). What may be noted here is the rejection of a role in practice for the theorist, because they operate outside of practice. (I should add that Walsh himself does not endorse this position; he merely describes it.) Various forms of action research (cf. Elliott, 1991) subscribe to this viewpoint.[29]

This perspective understands practice as deliberative action concerned with the making of appropriate decisions about practical problems *in situ*. This does not mean that there is no theoretical activity involved in the making of these decisions. What it does imply is that theoretical activity cannot apply only to technical decisions about how to implement theory developed by outsiders. It is not just that practitioners need to deliberate about the most efficient means to achieve certain pre-defined ends, it is the ends themselves which are subject to the deliberative process. Practice situations are not only particularistic, 'they are characterised by a complexity and uncertainty which resist routinization' (Usher et al., 1996, p. 127). Understanding of them needs to be continually formulated and reformulated by practitioners working in situ. In short, such knowledge is not propositional, which means that it always involves action and deliberation.

This standpoint leaves us with a number of problems. Adopting it has certain consequences, one of which is the difficulty of conceptualising it without resorting to timeless truths about its nature. Operating in a non-technicist way demands that practitioners do not behave as objective theorists say they should. But this reconceptualising of the relationship between theory and practice is itself theoretical and moreover theoretical in a normative sense. This dilemma can only be resolved by accepting the need for theoretical knowledge, which means that it has to refer to something. This is indeed Usher et al.'s (1996) solution as they accept that there is a place for theory in practical discourse, which of course in turn closely ties together theory and practice. For them, informal theory central to practice 'is situated theory both entering into and emerging from practice' (Usher et al., 1996, p. 35).

This leads to a fifth position, which is that the theorist and the practitioner are actually engaged in different activities. This more closely fits with Walsh's view when he argues that the nature of theorising practice demands the identification of four different discourses, each of which has implicit within it a distinctive way of understanding a practical field such as education and each of which is a legitimate activity. Walsh (1993, p. 44) suggests that there are four mutually supporting kinds of discourse, which he designates as 'deliberation in the strict sense of weighing alternatives and prescribing action in some concrete here and now . . . evaluation, also concrete, and at once closely related to deliberation and semi-independent of it . . . science, which has a much less direct relationship to practice . . . and utopianism, being the form of discourse in which ideal visions and abstract principles are formulated and argued over'. Discourse, he defines, as 'a sustained and disciplined form of enquiry, discussion and exposition that is logically unique in some significant way' (ibid., p. 53). However, he also acknowledges that discourses may be symbiotic with other types of discourses and thus logically can be clustered. The utopian discourse is understood as prescriptive and general; the deliberative as prescriptive and particularistic; the scientific as general and descriptive; and the evaluative as particularistic and descriptive. The consequence of this is that the theorist and the practitioner are operating in different ways and with different criteria as to what constitutes knowledge.

Practitioner Error

Each of these last two positions prioritises the contextual and the local in the determination of practitioner knowledge. However, it is important to emphasise that this does not mean that practitioners cannot be misguided about their practice. If this was so, then judgements about what is good practice could not be made because all types of practice would be equally good. What are the types of errors which practitioners could make? First, they could be misguided about appropriate ends. It is possible to argue that a school – a combination of various individual practices – which chooses to marginalise (by various forms of streaming or setting) certain groups of children, because it feels that the majority of children will suffer unless they do, has chosen poorly as to which ends it should pursue. To some extent, these ends are in fact means, with the real ends having been decided by policy makers. This is because a school has limited control over its allocative and authoritative resources.[30] Means and ends are here becoming entangled and cannot be thought of as discrete.

The second form of error made by an individual or a school comprises wrongly identified means to perfectly conceived ends. The recently introduced literacy and numeracy hours in United Kingdom primary schools are examples of this. The ends are perfectly conceived – that is they are designed to raise the standards of literacy and numeracy for all children. However, the means may be misguided for a number of reasons. The technologies underpinning the new numeracy and literacy curricula may have been poorly conceived. Equally, there may be unexpected and unplanned consequences of the imposition of such curricula, ie. children develop a technical facility in reading and number work at the expense of a deep understanding of either of these activities which might mean that reading and number work in later life are neglected.[31] A child can be technically adept at these basic skills without having the inclination to use them at a later point in time. Another consequence might be that because the introduction of new numeracy and literacy programmes is time-consuming, other more worthwhile ends (and what is considered to be more worthwhile can only be decided in terms of appropriate curricula aims) are neglected or distorted. This is perhaps what we might want to call planned or expected consequences of the introduction of new curricula. A third example is that since teachers are centrally implicated in the delivery of any curriculum, the introduction of a new curriculum imposed by government may result in poorer performance in delivering the whole curriculum, or disruption to the coherence of what it replaced, or disturbance to the pedagogical routines of the teacher (and these might include the types of relations established and negotiated between teachers and pupils, the balance between the different skills, aptitudes and content domains of that curriculum and so forth). Means directed towards good ends therefore may be poorly conceived either because the technology itself is faulty or because there are planned consequences which impact upon other ends to their detriment or more likely because there are unexpected consequences of the implementation of those means.[32]

The third type of practitioner error is where the practitioner simply does not have the skills or the opportunities or the resources to put efficiently into practice those means which have been identified as appropriate either by outsiders or by the practitioner. However, if, as we suggested above, the teacher is centrally implicated in the delivery of any curriculum, then that curriculum cannot be understood apart from the skills, dispositions, understandings and perceptions of those individual teachers, and the contexts in which they have to operate. There is, we can perhaps suggest, no such thing as a teacher-proof curriculum. Despite this difficulty, it is still surely correct to argue that some teachers have a better understanding of their own practice than others, that some teachers are better able to develop their skills than others and even that, given the considerable constraints on teachers, some are better able to make use of those limited resources than others. So even if we want to understand the curriculum as in part comprising particular dispositions of teachers, we are still in a position to make a judgement about the way it is delivered; and this also means that it is possible to identify errors in practice.

The next question concerns who is most appropriately positioned to identify those errors. The process of remedying errors in practice comprises both an identification phase and an implementation phase; and, furthermore, certain ways of identifying errors in practice may not be appropriate if the purpose is to correct those errors and thus improve the practice. This is because it is difficult to identify correct procedures for implementing a curriculum when the teacher's role is so central to its delivery, and more importantly, there may be unexpected or unplanned consequences. An example of this is OFSTED inspections of schools in the United Kingdom. Inspection teams may or may not be able to identify good or bad schools or even good or bad teachers,[33] but the identification itself (ie. the process of inspection) may actually lead to a deterioration in practice (lower teacher morale, fewer resources, delimitations of teacher professionalism and so forth). Furthermore, teachers are positioned (and thus constrained) by various structural properties of the system and institutions in which they work, which affects both how they understand professional knowledge and how it impacts on their practice.

However, even if errors are identified and corrected and this leads to a state of affairs which is at odds with the original theoretical conception, this does not mean that it was wrong or even that the relationship between theory and practice which it assumed was in turn wrongly conceived. What it means is that particular configurations of structural properties in society at particular moments in time and place have meant that certain actors in the power game were not able to achieve their ends. Indeed, policy-makers are as much concerned with creating the conditions by which policy is received and acted upon as they are with creating that policy in the first place.[34] The real issue we need to confront is whether it is possible for an outsider, ie. non-practitioner, to develop theoretical precepts about practice which are binding on those practitioners because they constitute a superior form of knowledge to the knowledge developed by the practitioner working *in situ* (though they may choose to ignore them).

In a sense, the distinction between the logical and the practical that is being made here is itself untenable. This is because what is logical is to some extent derived from what actually is, or has been or could be. Practice itself, especially educational practice, has been constructed through inter-active games played by many actors throughout history and what we have now is a consequence of these games. In other words, how we consider and what conclusions we come to about the most appropriate relationship between theory and practice is a question of value, ie. it involves delibera-tion and argument about the purposes of the educational enterprise which cannot be derived from an a priori linguistic examination of the concept of education per se. Thus any model we propose about what are appropriate ends for education also implies a particular understanding of how those ends are to be implemented and of how the theory–practice relationship should be conceptualised. And this ultimately can be reduced to com-petition between different sets of values. We cannot logically derive a role for the outside theorist and indeed a role for the practitioner from an examination of the notion of education, though we may be able to derive such an understanding of these roles from particular values we hold about the educational enterprise.

This after all is what Macintyre (1988) meant by the notion of a practice or more accurately a tradition, because the latter embeds a practice within the way it has evolved. For Macintyre, within any historical moment there may be dominant traditions of thought, rival traditions which demand less allegiance and traditions which are going through epistemological crises. But these traditions cannot be subsumed under one overall notion of ration-ality. They are incommensurable, though it is possible to observe another tradition, even if from a different perspective. As Macintyre (1988, p. 356) himself argues, this means that 'we either have to speak as protagonists of one contending party or fall silent'. These traditions compete with each other as they imply different and conflicting notions of rationality. If they did not, then they would not strictly speaking be different. There would, in other words, only be right and wrong ways of seeing the world: 'but genuinely to adopt the standpoint of a tradition thereby commits one to its view of what is true or false and, in so committing one, prohibits one from adopting any rival standpoints' (Macintyre, 1988, p. 367). It is not that one party is more or less correct than another, or that members of one tradition understand rationality better than members of other traditions. Rival traditions are genuinely in competition with each other and cannot within their own way of life reach an agreement. That they may do so occurs because one or other of the parties has abandoned wholly or in part those precepts which constituted the tradition to which they formally belonged.[35]

What therefore are we to make of the notion of error, which has concerned us much in this chapter, especially in the light of its consideration within the criteria supplied by the tradition of knowledge within which it is embedded? We can certainly judge an error to have occurred if, in the light of those mores and codes, implementation of a curriculum does not produce desired for or expected outcomes (though we should be careful about how we measure those outcomes). Second, we may be able to subscribe to an idea of error more readily if it is identified by the maker him/herself. What we can do, however, is suggest appropriate conditions for practitioners to identify errors in their practice and ways of correcting those errors (and this may include a fundamental reconceptualisation of that practice itself) which have the best chance of being successfully sustained (ie. do not have deleterious consequences).

Professional Development

What is most striking over the last ten years is the effectiveness of governments in changing the infrastructure of practice. This has been achieved by changing the structures and contexts within which teachers work and equally by changing the discursive regimes within which they operate. In the first case, changing structures (for example, creating a quasi-market of educational achievement in the form of published league tables and imposing a National Curriculum)[36] have also had the effect of changing the knowledge base through which teachers operated and which underpinned decisions they made about curricula within their classrooms. This works by changing priorities, so that instead of teachers striving to meet the needs of all children in their classrooms, they are now concerned to maximise the achievements of those children who will have the most effect on the school's position in the league table. An inclusive policy has replaced an exclusive policy.[37] The point that is being made here is that practitioner knowledge may be affected (the question as to whether it has been adversely affected is different) by changes to the contexts in which teachers operate. Their notion of professional knowledge, comprising content, pedagogy, educational ends, educational means and their own role in the process, has necessarily been transformed by the way they now understand how they are positioned within these new structures. Of course, as we have suggested in previous chapters, structural properties do not determine how we think and behave, not least because those structural properties may be understood and interpreted in different ways by different practitioners. However, interpretations of structural properties are collectively mediated and negotiated within communities of fellow practitioners and these negotiations take place within contexts which position actors in terms of how they construct their own understandings; indeed, the way that they are positioned has been reformulated, which has had an effect on how they understand and prioritise means and ends in their own practice. Management structures which demand tighter accountability from practitioners may have the effect of discouraging teachers from experimenting within their classrooms.[38] Experimentation involves risk, which may in turn lead to failure which is now more tightly policed. In other words, the perceived sanctions attached to certain types of behaviours have been made more explicit and in some ways harsher, and this rationalisation has affected the way teachers behave.

The second way that governments over the last fifteen years have attempted to change professional knowledge is by changing the discursive regimes within which teachers operate and how they understand their own professionalism. This has been achieved in part by what Ball (1998) calls 'a discourse of derision', which has operated to marginalise sets of ideas which contradict those sets of ideas which government conceives to be correct.[39] Any view therefore of what constitutes professional practice needs to be contextualised within a set of institutional and discursive structures.

Professional development is defined here as the progressive development of appropriate skills or competencies. These skills or competencies may be logically related in that higher order competencies are accretions or more effective manifestations of lower order competencies (one becomes for instance a better teacher) or different order skills (one develops skills appropriate to management roles, for example). In the latter case, the lower order and higher order competencies are not logically related; indeed, the skills required to perform the first set of tasks are different from the skills required to perform the second set of tasks. These models are further complicated by the fact that individuals may both be acquiring skills and operating as teachers and managers and that they frequently operate with different and conflicting agendas in performing each role. The manager may therefore find that they are behaving competently in ways which have a negative impact on their other role as a teacher, and that development in the first capacity diminishes the capacity to develop in the second way. This happens because the two strands involve the acquisition of different sets of skills and have different aims and purposes.

We are concerned here with those competencies, skills and dispositions which are central to the professional development of the teacher. The model is 'ideal' – its purpose is aspirational – and ideological – it is underpinned by a particular set of values. It may be characterised in the following way: professional development involves the deliberate monitoring of one's actions, their evaluation and the development of solutions to problems which arise. This best takes place in settings which allow monitoring to be undertaken in conjunction with other people engaged in the same activity. This self-reflexive activity is understood as only able to be undertaken in certain kinds of environments. These may be characterised as epistemological, psychological and organisational.

In the first case this involves the creation of an environment which approximates to Habermas' (1987) ideal speech situation. For Habermas, statements about the world do not correspond to reality. We cannot establish facts about the world; we can only, in seeking knowledge, reasonably argue. What does he mean by this? The truth can be established, and it may only be an ideal, if in discourse, those elements which contribute to irrationality are excluded. This may seem to be tautological, but Habermas' twist on the dilemma allows a way out. If we can identify those elements which prevent us from reaching our ideal, we perhaps have a way of framing 'the pursuit of truth'. These elements would include relations of power between different protagonists.

In an educational institution, structured and differentiated as it is, with some people occupying positions of power and therefore by virtue of their positioning having a monopoly on resources, those with less power may feel constrained to express their views. So one principle would be that the consequences of arguing a case should not in any way be affected by other considerations. The communicative act is sealed off from the real world of differential positioning. However, we still have to confront a number of other problems and these comprise devices commonly used in language games. Rhetorical devices, such as concealment of position, irony, assertiveness, over-emphasis and the like have to be removed from the equation because some are more skilled at their use than others. The language game must be played so that protagonists have equal resources, and this applies also to the level of information each protagonist has to resolve the argument.

Rapidly, we are cloning our two players in the game, so that they are bound to agree by virtue of being the same. But this involves a misunderstanding of the nature of the game because all we are stripping away is those factors which comprise inequality and unfairness. Our two notional discussants coming from different positions, but without the impedimenta of differentiated positioning, may now debate and reach an agreement which is truly rational. Rationality therefore inheres in properly conducted discourse or communication. There are two consequences of this approach. First, though Habermas is defending rationality, his defence is not that of equating it with reality. Rational agreement comprises consensus achieved when all the constraints to reaching such an agreement have been removed. Second, his approach is critical and emancipatory in that the 'ideal speech situation' is literally that and impediments to it need to be examined and then dissolved. Furthermore, knowledge of those impediments (structural/ ideological inequalities) goes some way to meeting these demands.[40]

Furthermore, it allows the teacher to engage in the process of knowledge creation. Shulman (1987, p. 8) suggests that there are seven broad areas of knowledge which require examination by the teacher. These are: content knowledge; general pedagogical knowledge, with special reference to those broad principles and strategies of management and organisation that appear to transcend the subject matter; curriculum knowledge, with particular grasp of the materials and programmes that serve as 'tools of the trade' for teachers; pedagogical content knowledge, that special amalgam of content and pedagogy that is uniquely the province of teachers, their own special form of professional understanding; knowledge of learners and their characteristics; knowledge of educational contexts, ranging from the workings of the group to the character of communities and cultures; and knowledge of educational ends, purposes and values, and their philosophical and historical grounds. These are epistemological desiderata for professional development.

The second of our contexts is psychological. Rogers (1967) emphasises the need to create the right conditions to facilitate the development of a person's inherent ability to understand themselves in a positive way. He identifies these conditions as: unconditional positive regard; understanding of one's internal frame of reference; and the opportunity to communicate this understanding/experience to others. Given Rogerian conditions, the developing person has the capacity to reorganise their self-perception and acquire a more positive sense of self, and thus enhance their self-esteem. Defining self-esteem is not unproblematic. Lawrence (1988) places it within the umbrella term of 'self concept' which is composed of three aspects: self-image, ideal self and self-esteem. He then defines self-image as an individual's picture of their characteristics formed through the process of social interaction; ideal self as an image of what s/he should be; and self-esteem as her/his appraisal of the discrepancy between these two. The Self-Esteem Network (1997, p. 3) identifies nine elements of self-esteem: unconditional self-acceptance; sense of capability; sense of purpose; appropriate assertiveness; experience of flow and fulfilment; sense of responsibility and accountability; sense of safety and security; sense of belonging; sense of integrity. These reflect Rogers' (1983) description of what it is to be a person: openness to experience; trust in one's organism; having an internal locus of evaluation and a capacity to change. These capacities are better developed through some organisational structures than others.

The third of our contexts is therefore organisational, and it is here that the most difficult dilemmas for educational administrators lie. I have already suggested that those concerned to support professional development in institutions should: create the best possible conditions for deliberation about professional practice; remove structural inequalities, for example, gender discrimination, from the process of deliberation; allow opportunities to focus on those areas which characterise the professional role; and create the conditions which best allow those psychological dispositions which facilitate human growth to flourish. Furthermore, these conditions do not preclude disagreement, vigorous debate and argument. Indeed, a characteristic of this organisation is respect for persons and their different value systems.

This may be contrasted with an entrepreneurial model of educational management in which the organisation requires its members to work to common and predetermined goals and is characterised by their efficient achievement. The professional is conceived of as a technician whose role is to meet targets set by other people, but has little direct input into the formulation of those goals. As Smyth (1993, p. 7) suggests:

> What occurs, of course, is a cultural shift away from education to management and other forms of entrepreneurialism. We lose sight of what it is that is being managed and what we have is the replacement of a professional model of education with what is a largely discredited industrial management model. Why we in education would want to emulate this kind of derelict model that failed so demonstrably as evidenced in the corporate excesses of the 1980s is a complex mystery.

What is being suggested here is that a form of professional development can take place in an entrepreneurial institution, but that it is likely to be superficially conceived, concerned with career advancement and the enhancement of personal esteem and ultimately inefficient. That is, an entrepreneurial agenda may restrict the practitioner's capacity to engage in a process of professional development as it is described here.

Two further points need to be made. The first concerns the relationship between the educational institution and the system within which it is positioned. Certain types of accountability relations act to restrict the types and modes of professional development which can operate, and this is most obviously apparent in the changes that OFSTED inspections have brought to schools and teacher training institutes. The second point is related and suggests that even with accountability relations that seek to deny practitioners the opportunities to develop their professional understanding, there is still space within the system to subvert those agendas which threaten it.

The first part of this book has been concerned with the development of a theory of educational knowledge which set out particular ontological, epistemological and methodological positions and the relations between them. The second part of this book examines a number of issues with reference to the framework developed above.

Part 2
Disciplinary Knowledge

6 School Effectiveness Research

One of the most influential educational discourses of the 1990s is 'school effectiveness/school improvement'.[41] It is important to keep the two separate, though attempts have been made to draw them closer together (Gray et al., 1996).[42] School effectiveness research has its origins in a general dissatisfaction with the 'deterministic' and 'pessimistic' view of schooling which suggested that schools, teachers and education generally have little effect on the different ways different pupils perform in schools. Other background factors are more influential and there is little schools can do to counteract their effects. Though leading practitioners (ie. Sammons et al., 1995, p. 80) recognise that school effectiveness findings cannot provide a blueprint for school improvement, they argue that 'such research provides a valuable background and useful insights'. Though this assertion seems to offer a way forward, it is important to note here that it operates in a purely polemical sense, and this is partly because the nature of the relationship is not made sufficiently explicit for any reader to act on it so as to produce any useful outcomes. What is needed is an understanding of the relationship between sets of precepts about educational effectiveness developed by non-practitioners and practical knowledge or phronesis which guides the actions of practitioners. Furthermore, we may also need to surface the implicit power relations which operate between researchers making claims about what an effective school is and practitioners concerned to modify and improve their practice in the light of specifications about how they should behave.

Sammons et al. (1995) make the following claims:

- Although socio-economic factors and innate dispositions of students are major influences on achievement, schools 'in similar circumstances can achieve very different levels of educational progress' (p. 83).
- There are some studies which suggest that both academic and social/ affective outcomes such as attendance, attitudes and behaviour are effected by the school. In other words, children attended more, truanted

less, had better attitudes towards schooling and behaved better whilst at school in the more effective schools compared with the less effective.

- Primary schools can have significant long-term effects on achievement at 16 years of age.
- It is possible to measure the difference which schools make. Creemers (1994, p. 13) for example, suggests that 'about 12 to 18 per cent of the variance in student outcomes can be explained by school and classroom factors when we take account of the background of the students'.
- Prior achievement is a much more significant factor than gender, socio-economic, ethnicity and language characteristics and even that school effects are more important than these characteristics but not that of prior attainment.
- There is some evidence that school effects vary for different kinds of outcomes, ie. mathematical as compared with language achievements.
- The amount of variance in achievement attributable to schools and classes may vary from culture to culture.
- There is no simple combination of factors which can produce an effective school.

Definitions of Effectiveness

One of the most contentious aspects of the discourse is the definition of effectiveness. Mortimore (1992) has suggested that an effective school is one 'in which students progress further than might be expected from consideration of its intake'; and conversely 'in an ineffective school students make less progress than expected given their characteristics at intake'. This definition attempts to do three things. First, it suggests that it is possible to determine (we will leave aside for the moment the question of whether it is possible to measure these characteristics) what those ends are which students progress towards. Second, it assumes a mono-linear view of the relationship between learning and student characteristics at entry to either the school or the school system; or in other words, a student's progress is determined in a straightforward linear fashion by certain factors, albeit that those factors and the relations between them operate within a framework of probability. Goldstein (1998) has claimed that it is now possible to plot the different ways those background variables impact on the learning experiences of children. Despite advances in statistical techniques, mathematical modelling is only able to deal with those background influences by processing them in particular ways. An example could be the effects of one-family parenthood on children's development and this is assumed to be the same for all children of one-parent families. Though it is now possible to plot changes in family status over time, what it is not possible to do is to model mathematically the different ways family status impacts on individual children at different points in their lives. The relationship has to be expressed in a linear fashion to meet the methodological demands of such modelling. Social class attributes (as measured by parental employment), particular forms of school organisation, classroom pedagogies and the like have an effect on the learning capacities of children in distinctive ways. Third, it suggests that values are not an important dimension of school effectiveness research. Again, we will return to this but for now it is worthwhile to suggest that gender, social class, styles of teaching, management strategies are all value-rich concepts – that is they do not operate as descriptive terms, but operate to impose a particular way of ordering on the world. They are thus ideological constructions and need to be understood as such.

We now come to the central concern of the matter which is whether school effectiveness researchers have successfully defined their task so as to preclude accusations that they simply seek to impose a particular value position on the study of schools. In Chapter 4 it was suggested that mathematical modelling, a favoured research strategy of school effectiveness researchers, does in fact carry with it a good measure of ideological baggage. Indeed, it is important to address whether from the outset school effectiveness researchers have failed to satisfy their self-professed desire for value-free knowledge of schooling by using the notion of effectiveness. White (1997) thinks that they have not. His argument is that the notion of effectiveness carries with it two meanings. The first is a purely instrumental function; that is, regardless of what we seek to do, effectiveness refers to whether we have achieved our purpose. The second meaning is more significant. This argues that we cannot separate out means and ends in any simplistic way, especially with regards to education. Now it is perfectly logical to suggest that a school could be effective and yet still produce outcomes which may be considered to be undesirable. Indeed, Reynolds (1985) would agree with this, as he does in his discussion of some of the early American research into school effectiveness: 'there is an absence of any philosophical discussion of what schools ought to be doing and an uncritical acceptance of high achievement test scores as the education system's only goal'. School effectiveness researchers would therefore still want to argue that effectiveness is something which we would want our schools to be concerned with, but they would add the rider that we have to make sure that our ends are ethically justifiable. After all, it would hardly make sense to suggest that educators would want to meet their aims ineffectually, thus rendering the subsequent educational programme inadequate.

White (1997, pp. 42–43), however, argues that 'the fact that measures to make less effective schools more effective are labelled "school improvement" blurs the distinction still further between "good as a means" and "good more generally"'. He goes on to suggest that 'while both "improvement" and "progress" could be understood in a value-neutral, means-end sense, as implying getting closer to the ends in question, however good or bad they were, they usually have more global connotations' (ibid.). What does he mean by the phrase 'global connotations'? He means that while specific aims may be achieved by the adoption of a neutral and value-free mechanism, the operation of that mechanism may indeed have other consequences, both easily foreseen but also unpredictable. An example will bring out the force of the argument. If our goal is simply the teaching of the ten times table, then though with the majority of children this can be achieved using benign and humane methods, in some cases it may be necessary (as it was considered to be in the past) to employ coercive measures. The end is now efficiently achieved, but the use of these coercive measures with some pupils may have far-reaching consequences for their development. So we can see here that the means-end distinction inherent in the definition of school effectiveness is not quite as simple as it seems. It is the relationship between a variety of ends – and ends which as educators we may not foresee – which determines the precise means we employ. Furthermore, the means we employ embody particular value perspectives. It is not just that we have to decide about appropriate means for value-impregnated ends, we also have to decide about the appropriate balance, as we understand it, between ends and means, and this can only be determined by our conception of how society should be structured and this of course is an ideological or value-laden enterprise.[43]

Brown et al. (1995) suggest another way in which values seep in, almost unnoticed. The methods employed by school effectiveness researchers assume a hierarchically stratified model of a school comprising nested layers of systems within systems.[44] Classrooms are nested within subject departments which are in turn nested within schools. They write that:

> The model does, of course, have a common-sense logic if the way one sees the world of education is essentially one of top down management and a common feature of writing on school effectiveness is the clear implication that it is necessary for a subject department to be nested within a school that is managed effectively if it is to be effective.
>
> (ibid., p. 8)

The implication of this is that the conceptualisation of the relations between different phenomena which is methodologically central to school effectiveness research strategies does in fact comprise a view of how a school should be organised. In short, those strategies are informed by a set of values which are distinctively normative in character.

Furthermore, if we examine one of the key characteristics of effective schools, we may be able to understand why Ball and others have suggested that what is being offered by school effectiveness researchers is in effect a managerial discourse and one, moreover, which is 'also couched in an ideology of neutrality' (Ball, 1998, p. 133). We are told (cf. Sammons et al., 1995) that an effective school needs professional leadership. Indeed, Gray (1991) argues that 'the importance of the head teacher's leadership is one of the clearest of the messages from school effectiveness research'. However, it is more difficult to determine what exactly this characteristic is. It is certainly not 'weak'. It may involve 'assertive leadership and quality monitoring' (Scheerens, 1992). It frequently comprises: '1) strength of purpose; 2) involving other staff in decision-making; 3) professional authority in the processes of teaching and learning' (Sammons et al., 1995, p. 90). It may consist of 'vigorous selection and replacement of teachers' (Levine and Lezotte, 1990) and so forth.

Though the suggestion is for greater participative decision-making, elsewhere it is suggested that the head teacher should be the leading professional. Though on the surface these two characteristics would seem to be perfectly compatible, what as a reader we are not provided with is the context within which such participative leadership is exercised. These characteristics are allowed to float free from the real mechanisms which underpin schooling. Schools are hierarchically organised; that is, some players in the game have more power than others and furthermore those players with less power make decisions about how they should behave in terms of their understanding of those hierarchical structures within which they are positioned.[45] The point is that the research strategies adopted are implicitly positioned within a model of schooling which denies the existence of real structural properties (indeed the strategies themselves are incapable of addressing these issues, see Chapter 4); and though the language used is democratic, this acts to conceal the real relations within which teachers and pupils are embedded. In short, school effectiveness research is a normative model of educational knowledge which embraces research techniques for controlling the activities of teachers, while at the same time concealing its true identity.

Equity

School effectiveness researchers make two claims which on the surface seem to be entirely plausible. The first of these is that they are committed to a vision of equity. For example, Sammons et al. (1995, pp. 6–7) suggest that 'in terms of underlying vision, the concept of equity – raising the achievement of all students regardless of background characteristics such as sex, ethnicity or socio-economic status – has been the driving force in both UK and USA studies in the field'. The second claim they make is that they cannot be responsible for policy-makers 'cherry-picking what they wish to use in order to help legitimate their policies' (Goldstein and Myers, 1997, p. 1), and thus they refute the charge that 'school effectiveness research . . . has assisted in the process of governmental centralisation and control of education and educational professionals' (ibid.). We will see later how these two charges are in fact related.

The first charge is that school effectiveness research is committed to a distorted view of the equity debate, one moreover which emphasises equality of opportunity at the expense of equality of outcome (cf. Elliott, 1998). There are a number of positions which can be taken on this issue. The first position is underpinned by a belief that people are unequally talented because of their genetic predispositions. Improving social and educational conditions cannot ameliorate or change this state of affairs. Resources should therefore be targeted at the more talented, because in order for the less talented to be able to enjoy some measure of esteem in society, that society has to be organised in the most efficient way possible. Furthermore, because the most talented are the driving force behind the provision of esteem for the less talented, then they should be better rewarded, not least to motivate them to work harder so that the less talented are provided with the means to achieve that measure of self-esteem. The consequences of this viewpoint are a differentiated system of schooling and the targeting of different teaching programmes for different types of children (ie. the more talented and the less talented). Since the measure is a genetic one, various safety devices (ie. later rather than earlier assessment of ability) have to be set in place to ensure that talent is both recognised and rewarded. Furthermore, if it is deemed that recognition by those less talented of their talentless status would not contribute to the maintenance of their self-esteem, then this should be concealed from them. It should be noted here that this distinction is an ontological one, since it rests on a perception that human beings have fixed and innate intellectual dispositions.

The second position is underpinned by a similar belief, ie. people are unequally talented because of their genetic predispositions, but should be educated to their highest possible level. Even if that educational provision is effective, and in theory it is possible to make it so, this will not then lead to equality of outcome, because that is an ontological impossibility. Furthermore, since we are dealing with two sets of conditions: societal influences and educational provision, in order to maximise the education of talent to its fullest degree, both issues have to be addressed. Because social and genetic influences act to produce inequality of learning disposition, unequal provision or at least differentiated provision needs to be provided for children with different levels of talent and more importantly different levels of 'cultural capital' (Bourdieu and Passeron, 1980). Meanwhile, social programmes are required to even out the different levels of cultural capital acquired by children outside the school, even though this will have only a limited effect. There are two reasons for this. The first is genetic predisposition (children therefore learn at different rates) and the second is that however successful the ameliorative programmes in society are, they will never produce equality of cultural capital and thus some children's needs will always be different from others.

The third position introduces a new principle – that of merit. People are equally talented and therefore equally capable of benefiting from education, but some make less effort than others, and therefore abiding by the principle of natural justice, they deserve to be less well rewarded. A distinction needs to be made here between those dispositions which are in the control of the individual and those outside of his or her control. This is a difficult distinction to make. However, advocates of this strategy need to make it because it provides a justification for the unequal distribution of goods. What tends to happen with this position is that an assumption is made that it is possible to distinguish between the two and that schooling is understood as a testing ground for this strategy, so that those who work hard, regardless of the social conditions which structure their learning and their lives outside school, succeed at school and therefore deserve to be better rewarded than those who do not. As an essential precondition for the successful implementation of this strategy is a need to adopt ameliorative programmes which allow the successful flowering of those dispositions such as effort, diligence, hard work and so forth. A meritocracy requires that the means to the effective exercise of these virtues is not constrained by social and educational factors. Furthermore, although it acknowledges that schools have a part to play in this equalising of life chances, it also understands schooling as testing beds for these virtues. At this point it is perhaps pertinent to suggest that the second role for educational institutions, that is their role as providers of opportunities for the exercise of the virtues mentioned above, needs to be equally resourced for all children.

Our final position takes a different form. Poverty and other types of social disadvantage may have an effect on disposition to learn, not just because resources at home are likely to be limited, but also because poverty may lead to the adoption of short-term goals (acquiring the basic necessities of life) which may limit educational aspirations. Again, two consequences follow from this. The first is that educational provision should be both differentiated and unequally resourced in favour of those children who are less advantaged. Second, proponents of this position argue that equality of outcome is theoretically possible and that what prevents this happening is the way society is organised. Institutional reform (schools, families, communities) is therefore needed.

School effectiveness researchers tend to operate, albeit implicitly, within a framework which emphasises our third position. Because the school is identified as the prime mover in educational achievement and because little attention is paid to the socially constructed nature of the curriculum taught in schools, then schools are understood as operating outside of those networks of power which act to produce certain types of children and which are socially and culturally located. Thus by sanctioning a model of schooling which allows comparisons to be made between schools, and by implicitly downgrading the effects of communities and society at large, we are left with an impoverished model of the relationship between schools and society, and an inadequate position in relation to the equity debate.

Political Collaboration

The claim that school effectiveness researchers cannot be held responsible for the thrust of government policy is one repeatedly made by leading advocates (cf. Goldstein and Myers, 1997). On the surface at least, it is clear that they cannot be held responsible for government officials, ie. politicians, civil servants and the like, misusing their findings and misrepresenting their arguments. For example, Goldstein and Myers (ibid., p. 1) argue that 'many research discussions have been quoted out of context, eg. OFSTED's work on reading (OFSTED, 1996) has sought to justify some dubious "research" by appealing to aspects of the School Effectiveness literature . . . and the literary task force report produced by the Labour Party sought to justify its comparisons among primary schools by questionable references to "intake adjustments"'. However, this is to miss the point of the argument which is three-fold. First, school effectiveness research has at its heart the desire to compare schools with each other in terms of a notion of hierarchy and normalisation (see Chapter 10). This is achieved by the application of a reductionist methodology which seeks through statistical methods to isolate a particular unit of social life, ie. the school, in order to then compare one example of the unit with another. If a notion of comparison is therefore sanctioned and this notion logically has attached to it a notion of hierarchy, ie. one unit is better or worse than another, however sophisticated the means for making that judgement, then what follows and is given credence is the idea that the reason for one school being worse than another is the responsibility of the teachers within it. This contributes to a culture of blame. There is, in other words, no proper systemic analysis of the relationship between schooling and society in school effectiveness research.

The second part of the argument has been referred to in Chapter 4 and this comprises the idea that it incorporates a reductionist methodology which determines how it is viewed and how the discourse is constructed, and which in the process marginalises debates about the aims and objectives of education. What is at issue in short is that a method from within a positivist/empiricist framework, which as we suggested in Part 1 is flawed, cannot help but provide support for an agenda which emphasises control, prediction and the rejection of an holistic view of education. Fielding (1997, p. 138) makes the following point: 'a major concern is that, for whatever reason, there seems to be a distressing blindness to the ideologically and epistemologically situated nature of its own intellectual position'.

Elliott (1996, p. 208) describes it as linked to an 'ideology of social control'. Notwithstanding replies to Elliott (Sammons and Reynolds, 1997), to Hamilton (Mortimore et al., 1997) and to a series of contributors to a volume called *Perspectives on School Effectiveness and School Improvement* (Mortimore and Sammons, 1997), these criticisms have not been effectively rebutted. Though they offer protestations to the effect that their ideological position is not 'social Darwinist' or 'eugenic' (Hamilton, 1997), it embraces a model which epistemologically and ontologically is in tune with those of UK governments of recent times.

The third part of the argument is that school effectiveness researchers by the adoption of the methodology they favour, ignore the contextual, the historical and the social. Again Fielding (1997, p. 143) suggests that 'its pre-occupation with "what works" ignores the question of whose interests shape the nature and process of the work. There is no recognition of the problematic nature of curriculum or of the possibility that schooling may be organised in the interests of, for example, dominant ethnic groups, males or the ruling classes.' Indeed, the socially situated nature of the discourse, which at the same time seeks to conceal its sociality, is deficient with regards to how knowledge of self and others is constructed by society and through schools.

School Effectiveness Factors

We now need to turn to the way school effectiveness researchers produce lists of factors which contribute to effectiveness. Levine (1992) argues that schools which are effective in value-added terms show the following characteristics: productive school climate and culture; focus on student acquisition of central learning skills; appropriate monitoring of student progress; practice-orientated staff development at the school site; outstanding leadership; salient parent involvement; effective instructional arrangements and implementation; and high operationalised expectations and requirements for students. In a similar way, Sammons et al. (1995) suggest that the following interdependent factors are significant:

1 Professional leadership (firm and purposeful; a participative approach; the leading professional).
2 Shared vision and goals (unity of purpose; consistency of practice; collegiality and collaboration).
3 A learning environment (an orderly atmosphere; an attractive working environment).
4 Concentration on teaching and learning (maximisation of learning time; academic emphasis; focus on achievement).
5 Purposeful teaching (efficient organisation; clarity of purpose; structured lessons; adaptive practice).

6 High expectations (high expectations all round; communicating expectations; providing intellectual challenge).
7 Positive reinforcement (clear and fair discipline; feedback).
8 Monitoring progress (monitoring pupil performance; evaluating school performance).
9 Pupil rights and responsibilities (raising pupil self-esteem; positions of responsibility; control of work).
10 Home–school partnership (parental involvement in children's learning).
11 A learning organisation (school-based staff development).

Such lists of specifications produced by school effectiveness researchers have been criticised on a number of grounds, and these need to be examined. The principal criticism is that they are tautological and associated in some people's minds with this is that they are trivial. These two points need to be treated separately. This is because they may not be tautological but they still may be trivial, and equally, they may be tautological but not trivial. Both criticisms are rejected by Goldstein and Myers (1997). First, they argue that it involves a misunderstanding of the nature of empirical investigation and second, they claim that the findings are not logically trivial per se. It should be noted at this stage of the argument that they have conflated the two criticisms set out above so that it is difficult to counteract them because as a consequence they do not address the essential problem.

As we will see, triviality only denotes that our understanding of educational systems is superficial – not necessarily that it is wrong. Tautological insufficiency denotes that, though such understanding seems to be derived from empirical study, in fact it is derived from reasoning from definitions. As White (1997, p. 45) argues in his discussion of Sammons et al.'s third factor (see above) 'an orderly learning environment':

> For children to learn from teachers, certain conditions must – logically must – be satisfied. The learners must pass from a state of not-knowing to a state of knowing. To reach this, their teachers must draw their attention to the subject matter to be learnt and correct their mistakes so that they come to have a better understanding. This requires some sort of organised, planned activity on the part of the teacher. All this is a part of what we understand by teaching. If classrooms were always in chaos, those organised teaching activities would be, by definition, ruled out.

On first sight this argument would seem to have some merit. However, what is orderly may be understood in a number of different ways. Indeed, what is understood by teaching and learning may be construed in different ways. To suggest that learning can only take place when the teacher–learner relationship is characterised by an organised and planned programme of activities (and therefore by implication what is intended to be taught, if it is taught effectively, is per se what is learnt) presupposes that intention is not responsive to outcomes at different stages of the programme and cannot therefore comprise elements of spontaneity which are not accounted for in the original preparation. However, be that as it may, we can still say that chaos – that is the absence of circumstances in which communication between teacher and student is possible – is a logically necessary condition for effective teaching. But this is an extreme example. There are a number of positions between chaos and order which it is reasonable to suggest may or may not be conducive to effective learning and therefore may be investigated empirically.[46] The problem is not that Sammons et al.'s factor is tautological or that it is logically trivial, but that it is ill-defined and as a consequence as a descriptive device trivial per se.

This points to the principal problem with identifying such outcomes, and this is that in order to establish an association between different factors (and we have to remember that Sammons et al.'s list of factors are interdependent) and good outcomes, we have to define our terms so that one orderly learning environment as it is observed is like, in all essential respects, other orderly learning environments so that the comparison we make is fair. If like is not compared with like because we are dealing with a singularly ill-defined concept, then our claim about any associational property we may think we have discovered cannot be sustained.

Field Construction

This chapter has made reference to the argument developed in the first part of the book. To reiterate: values are central to the activity of research, that is both the values of the researcher and the values of those being researched. Research, therefore, is inevitably a 'fusion of horizons' (Gadamer, 1975), in which different sets of values fuse to produce new knowledge. These values, or conceptual frameworks, are located within historical contexts or 'traditions of knowledge' (Macintyre, 1988). The production of knowledge, therefore, has a close relationship with the way society organises itself. However, to understand knowledge and power as inseparable (cf. Chapter 10) is to erect too rigid a straightjacket on the relationship between social arrangements and knowledge (both about them and other matters). I now want to extend this argument to the realm of curricula or to the way knowledge is produced and reproduced in educational institutions by examining one aspect of the process – the way knowledge is organised (its boundary definitions). The argument, I will suggest, is that the way we divide up knowledge has an effect on the way we can and do understand the world.

Each discursive field[47] (I am using this term to describe a specific demarcation or boundary point between domains of knowledge) has a history, is composed of individuals with different projects who form and re-form in different alliances at different moments. There are therefore, micro-political struggles within the history of each field. But, more importantly, at the level of the academy, those struggles involve the establishment of various organs of dissemination and of criteria by which the knowledge-producing activity may be judged. In the first place, a new field needs to produce books and articles in academic journals; new journals which reflect the epistemological assumptions of the field; positions of office in universities; access to the popular media; the development of a cadre of taught and research students; research funding for projects; and the establishment of a coterie of referees for journals and research projects. The paraphernalia of field formation is often hard-won, frequently involves excursions down blind alleys, and is a risk-taking business.

But more importantly, the field needs to establish three sets of criteria before it can be considered to be fully formed: first, it has to have created a set of criteria by which its knowledge may be evaluated; second, it needs to have formalised a set of definitional criteria which includes and excludes what is considered proper knowledge; third, it needs to be able to offer a set of methodological criteria with which an initiate may operate – a set of procedures which delineate a practitioner from a non-practitioner. Whilst some of these moves are more successful than others, they are, as Macintyre (1988) points out, always subject to decay, argument, dispute and change. The field itself always has to operate within other discursive fields, for example, the wider field of policy. Macro-political influences, therefore, have an influence on the way the field comes into being, and indeed practitioners (especially in the field of education) may deliberately shape their thinking to chime with policy moves, either actually in existence or projected.

Two examples will suffice. The first is ethnography, not understood as a field in its own right, but as a sub-set of the wider field of methodology. Forty years ago, this would not have been considered appropriate as a knowledge-producing activity. It is now acceptable in the academy, as its organs of dissemination are now well enough established to sustain it as a serious activity. However, it is not acceptable within wider contexts such as policy-making forums, and practitioners are therefore weakened by their inability to participate in macro-political processes.

The second example is the school effectiveness/school improvement discourse which has been the focus of this chapter. The creation of such a discourse has come about as a result of a number of moves made by important players in universities: for example, the marginalisation of existing forms of knowledge, such as the sociology of education, the philosophy of education and curriculum studies. This process has been accomplished by the cementing of alliances between policy-making bodies such as the DfEE and the academic community; and more importantly, the setting in place by government of a number of apparatuses (eg. OFSTED Inspection, National League Tables, etc.) which better facilitate the successful operation of the discourse, and which at the same time act to circumscribe and set boundaries to the field. This has involved the creation of an uneasy alliance between school effectiveness researchers and school improvers. On the surface, this would seem to be incongruous since the two sets of theorists generally differ about those sets of methodological criteria which determine the nature of their knowledge base. However, the alliance has survived and has been sustained by an agreement about the nature of the relationship between theory and practice. In addition, the movement has sought to market itself and thus establish a bridgehead to the world of practitioners, ie. by the use of marketing devices and by sustaining close relationships with knowledge users.

These two examples, incomplete as they are as histories, suggest that knowledge in the academy represents a fluid configuration, which is always in a state of flux. Subsequent reconfigurations which may or may not be influenced by older typifications of knowledge, merely confirm the flexible and changing nature of knowledge typifications. However, as Foucault (1980) argues, these manoeuvres have material effects: that is, they open and close discursive possibilities, and limit and delimit what can be said about education. These reconfigurations are also in part influenced by policy-making processes and a discussion of these is the subject matter of the next chapter.

7 Education Policy

Three Versions of Policy Processes

In the past fifteen years education policy-makers have focused on changing the culture of schools. They have attempted to do this in three ways: the development of new structures for managing schools (both within and without); the establishment of consumerist and state control mechanisms of accountability (Kogan, 1986); and the endorsement of different arrangements for teaching and learning. Original intentions, however, rarely mirror eventual outcomes. Though the policy process is frequently understood as a one-way flow from centre to periphery in which a set of policies is conveyed along the chain and implemented, it is better thought of as fractured, dislocated, only occasionally exhibiting a linear form. At every stage – primary, secondary or recontextualising (Bernstein, 1985) – policy texts are worked on and undergo change.

The policy text therefore becomes a bricolage (Bowe et al., 1992), an overlay or series of overlays. At each stage of the process, the text is 'overwritten', but always within specific contexts. During the initial phase of making policy, different interests collide, but these interests are not equally positioned and therefore have different capacities for influencing policy outcomes. Ideas and texts are worked on at different moments by social actors operating within these contexts. At each site, the mechanism for making policy determines how texts are written, rewritten and over-written. Power operates, as Foucault (1980) argues, not as an overwhelming apparatus of the central authority but infused in every human deliberation.[48] However, privileged social actors can exert control over this process in a number of ways: they can alter the means by which policy texts are created; they can directly influence policy deliberations by personal interventions (cf. Graham and Tytler, 1993);[49] they can determine the agenda for discussion at the various sites; and they are in a unique position to influence secondary bodies, for example, the media, which structure what is acceptable in terms of actual and anticipated sets of ideas.

Policy deliberation though, is always a projection, and it literally has a political momentum to it. It is not just about what is deemed appropriate in practice, but also about what will work in different circumstances than exist at present. It is therefore a weighing-up of advantages and dis-advantages, and is located within other discourses – party political, media, etc. The process is supra-logical and can hardly be said to be authored as such, since the actual and anticipated contexts of policy-making are always in a state of flux.

This view of policy can be set against two others. In the first, the central authority, though frequently prepared to disguise its intentions, always operates to further the interests of capital (Hatcher and Troyna, 1994). Education policy is directed towards this end. Hidden forces control and direct policy, and these forces have an overwhelming logic to them.

There are a number of problems with this. Those in positions of power rarely operate with such a coherent view of policy. This hidden psycho-logical mechanism, this form of downward conflating of the socio-cultural and cultural systems (Archer, 1988), reduces the human actor to a plasticity that denies their ability to act intentionally and in effect excludes the pos-sibility of social actors influencing policy. In contrast, the impulsion that guides policy is supra-logical, because integral to it are the multi-authored nature of policy texts, and the vested interestedness of individual authors in their interventions. It therefore understands agency as always existing within contexts: those contexts being real and material, as well as ideal and projected. Policy deliberation therefore, is frequently about what is thought to be the case, as well as what is the case.

The other view of policy is the pluralist model, where the policy process is understood as driven by diversity, and influenced at every level by a variety of interests. In this version, policy texts are multi-authored and contested, causing adjustments to be made at every level. The completed text therefore, incorporates the views of a wide range of interests. This has the effect of creating a single text which alone can satisfy all the interests concerned. The textual logic is triumphantly reasserted, even if the text is multi-authored. However, all the relevant interests are not equally represented and social actors do not have equal chances of influencing the construction of these texts.

If we reject both of these views, we need to develop different understand-ings of the policy process. The policy text is never complete, but always allows itself to be written over at every stage of the process and at every level.[50] Social actors at these different sites compete to produce their version of the final text, but only occasionally in terms of a totalising view of policy. This is because parts of the text are contested without regard to other parts. Other parts, and relations between these parts, are argued over, but in dif-ferent ways and in different forums. The policy as a whole is rarely debated and discussed. Furthermore, as the policy text moves between sites, different sets of values operate. At the reconceptualising stage, with the media, for example, commercial interests predominate. At the school level, practical issues become more important.

Finally, the policy process is continuous, rather than cyclical, since it cannot be understood as a series of discrete stages (ie. formulation, reformulation and implementation). Furthermore, it is frequently driven by evaluations which are constructed within an ideological framework. This construction may involve the commissioning of evaluation instruments which tell a certain type of truth or the direct control over those evaluation instruments. It may also involve the central authority in controlling the ideological apparatus, so that only certain types of evaluative truths are allowed to influence policy deliberations. This is of course never achieved absolutely, again for three reasons: the central authority does not have full control over the ideological apparatus; it is an amalgam of different people with different life-histories; more importantly, players in the policy game have only a limited understanding of how the policy process works, and how these policy texts will be received at different moments and places.[51]

Reading Policy Texts

This way of understanding the policy process may be illustrated by examining National Curriculum assessment arrangements for England and Wales between 1988 and 1994. National Curriculum documents such as the Dearing Report (*The National Curriculum and its Assessment* (1993)) are examples of purposive texts designed to change curriculum, pedagogic and assessment practices in schools. Reading texts, though, are necessarily acts of re-creation (Eco, 1984; Crossman, 1980); and thus, within temporal and spatial contexts, these texts allow multiple readings. They are also interpreted and reinterpreted at different moments of use, as meanings and outcomes are contested (Bowe et al., 1992; Scott, 1991). This allows for the possibility of 'resistance' (Giroux, 1983) to the original aims or purposes embedded in those documents. Understanding the relationship between intended outcomes and realisation therefore always involves making sense of competing sets of meanings situated within specific events in the lifetime of institutions and systems.

Textual reading is only part of the process – a process that involves textual construction (the initial writing of the text), textual reconstruction (formulations and reformulations of sets of meanings by practitioners), and implementation (teacher strategies influenced by textual readings). As Bowe et al. (1992, p. 83) make clear:

> Policy texts are not closed, their meanings are neither fixed nor clear, and the 'carry over' of meanings from one policy arena and one

educational site to another is subject to interpretational slippage and contestation.

Indeed the policy process is not uni-directional. Decision making at the various sites impacts backwards and forwards along the chain, causing policy texts to be rewritten and then repositioned in the policy arena. Penney and Evans (1994, p. 34) argue that, as a result, the '"flow" of policy is undoubtedly both complex and uneven', both because there is this 'two-way flow of text and discourse' and because actors at different sites in the policy process have different degrees of influence and autonomy. Indeed actors make decisions in contexts not of their own making, though the decisions they make impact on future contexts and arenas of decision making. The composition, length and direction of each relay (Bernstein, 1985) therefore, will vary with each episode of policy-making.

Texts are differently constituted. In Barthes' (1975) words, aspects of these 'official' texts are 'readerly'. The textual meaning is unequivocal, not subject to interpretation, non-writerly and therefore prescriptive. The text compels certain forms of action and proscribes others. On the other hand, texts such as these are not uni-dimensional. So any text is likely to contain 'readerly' as well as 'writerly' aspects. In the latter case the text is so constructed that the reader is allowed interpretative space. His or her options are not foreclosed by the text.

Paradoxically, Barthes' dichotomised view of reading ignores the reader. As Cherryholmes (1988, p. 12) argues, 'prior understandings, experiences, codes, beliefs and knowledge brought to a text necessarily condition and mediate what one makes of it'. Therefore, the degree to which such passivity or industry resides in the text itself or in the decoder of that text can only be determined by addressing each particular case. What is certain is that the relationship between reader and text lies somewhere on a continuum between active interpretation and passive reception. Texts, therefore, have properties which allow creative interpretation to a greater or lesser extent. They thus allow multiple readings, and contain contradictions and disjunctions. The result is that the practitioner, who works within the textual framework, has to chose between these different meanings, because he or she cannot accommodate them all.

These meanings compete with other sources of meaning, which support or deny particular interpretations. They compete with other textual meanings gathered from, for example, school and LEA documents, academic commentaries, newspaper reports and so forth, and they compete with other texts which bear indirectly on the matter in hand – other educational texts and non-educational books and pamphlets. Meanings held by individual teachers are influenced by spoken as well as written sources, and the everyday interactive processes that teachers go through confirm, deny, enrich, impoverish and certainly may change meanings which in turn will influence actions. This is to place the reading of policy texts within its proper context, and to argue that full understanding of what influences practice cannot be achieved by textual analysis alone. Teachers do more than simply read official documents.

The implementation of a new policy in schools therefore has to be understood as a complex social process, within which meanings and actions are fragmented at different sites during the passage of ideas from policy-making to realisation. As a result it would be misleading to conceive of the policy process as a linear chain with strategies and technologies made at one site and implemented at another. Texts and their subsequent reconstructions are read differently at different moments of use.[52]

Structural and Interactional Influences

It is important to place these different readings in context, and in doing so give full weight to the respective roles played by agency and structure in the policy process. Teachers' initial textual readings or their initial confrontation with the ideas implicit in the new text draw upon both those internalised rules which actors reproduce in their day-to-day working lives and those structural resources which position actors within set frameworks. Those elements of structure that are relevant to the matter in hand condition, but do not determine, actors' responses (Archer, 1982). Initial textual readings give way to subsequent interpretations and reinterpretations of assessment processes, and all the various readings are implicated in the implementation and reimplementation of assessment and pedagogic strategies. The interplay between structure and agency is transformed into new forms of structure and agency, and produces, in Archer's word, 'elaboration', that is, both elaborated structure and transformed agency. This cycle of activity at different moments and in different guises influences the implementation of processes.

In short, textual readings are transformed at different moments and places within schools as teachers construct and reconstruct meanings. This fragmentation is only realisable because, as Wexler (1982, p. 279) puts it, there is within educational contexts a high degree of 'tenuousness, dysfunction, interruption and possibility'. These meanings, moreover, are in competition with meanings conveyed by other texts and by other discursive forms. They are tested in formal and informal forums in schools, and they are formulated and reformulated within situationally constraining and enabling contexts which may or may not be fully understood by participants. These rules and resources (Giddens, 1984) structure and condition these sets of ideas and subsequent actions.

In the context of the implementation of a new assessment system in schools, policy is determined in three ways: by agents' bodies and biographies; by agents operating in settings, which are not of their own

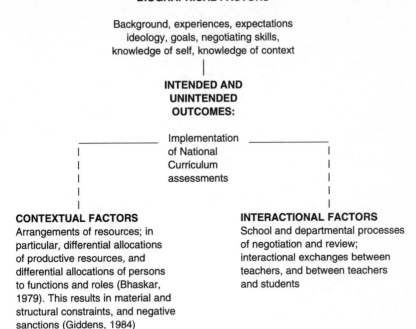

BIOGRAPHICAL FACTORS

Background, experiences, expectations
ideology, goals, negotiating skills,
knowledge of self, knowledge of context

**INTENDED AND
UNINTENDED
OUTCOMES:**

Implementation
of National
Curriculum
assessments

CONTEXTUAL FACTORS
Arrangements of resources; in
particular, differential allocations
of productive resources, and
differential allocations of persons
to functions and roles (Bhaskar,
1979). This results in material and
structural constraints, and negative
sanctions (Giddens, 1984)

INTERACTIONAL FACTORS
School and departmental processes
of negotiation and review;
interactional exchanges between
teachers, and between teachers
and students

Figure 7.1 Biographical, interactional and contextual factors in decision-making

making, but upon which they leave their mark; and within interactional
arenas which draw together agents and settings, and promote change (see
Figure 7.1). These result in both intended and unintended consequences
(that is, unintended both by individual, and collectivities of, agents) and
produce conformations and configurations of policy processes. Biographical
factors provide one type of context, material and structural factors another.
Examples of the latter are: differential allocation of persons to functions
and roles (Bhaskar, 1979); external constraints – examination technologies,
for example; teacher culture – subject hierarchies (cf. Goodson, 1985), professional codes and ideologies (Ball, 1982); conditions of work – arrangements of resources, pupil 'resistance' (Spradberry, 1976; Willis, 1977); and
institutional properties – devolved or centralised systems of decision-
making (Ball, 1987). Material, biographical and structural arrangements
therefore constitute the settings in which agents make decisions and formulate strategies, and in the process transform those arrangements. This is
because structure exists as both media and outcome of decisions made by
agents who could have acted in other ways. Archer (1982) argues that structures provide agents with good reasons for acting in the way they do, but
not overwhelmingly necessary ones. Thus the over-determination of much
sociological theorising is avoided.[53]

There are then two senses in which structure is used by sociologists. The first is the sense which Giddens gives to the term, that is arrangements of 'rules and resources'. Within schools there are both human and material resources. In the first place we have a group of differently resourced agents who interact in various ways. Their capacity to respond to any externally initiated change such as the introduction of a new assessment system in schools has both an internal element (biographical factors) and an external element (interactional and contextual factors). Though the two are separated here, this is artificial, because capacity is determined both by what actually is – arrangements of resources and rules at that precise moment and place – and how the agent perceives the situation. The actual balance between the two is an empirical matter and is determined by the knowledgeability of the agent. Agents though, perceive of themselves and act upon those perceptions in terms of publicly negotiated frameworks of meaning. Thus the teacher who is about to retire may be marginalised in decision-making arenas within the school because there is a feeling that the school needs to plan for the future (whether publicly expressed or not). Within a situation in which actors have different degrees of power and autonomy, the amount and type of power and autonomy they do have are dependent on the amount and type held by others.

But this is not a zero sum game, in which a finite and limited amount of power circulates between actors in particular social settings. First, the same actors may be differently related to each other in different situations. For example, a Head of House speaks with more authority on pastoral matters than a Head of Department, and conversely the latter has more influence over curriculum matters within his or her department than the Pastoral Head, who also may be a class teacher. What, of course, is a pastoral matter is as much a part of the negotiated frameworks of meaning that operate within institutions as any other matter; but it is important to emphasise that this process of negotiation is structured by arrangements of resources that we referred to earlier. Meanings are not negotiated between equals, but by differently resourced agents operating in differently arranged settings. In the last resort, this form of constraint derives its force from 'punitive responses on the part of some people towards others' (Giddens, 1984, p. 176). Second, and more important, those arrangements have implications for the amount and type of autonomy experienced by agents within their institutions. Third, some externally initiated projects empower some agents, whilst others empower different agents. Thus, government reforms to do with decentralising resource allocations empower head teachers; but reforms to the public examination system through the introduction of coursework empower individual teachers.

Material resources exert significant influences on human actions. Giddens' (1984, p. 76) characterisation of context operating as a form of constraint on human agents includes 'the character of the material world and . . . the physical qualities of the body'. Human agents cannot be in more than one place at any one time. The environment of the institution, its physical qualities, is the setting in which actors make decisions. Classes of students are allocated. Rooms operate to limit movement. The availability of books and other paper resources influences and restricts possible teaching approaches. In short, the arrangement of such resources is the context within which actors devise and implement teaching strategies.

Giddens' third type of constraint deriving from 'the contextuality of action, ie. from the "given" character of structural properties vis-a-vis situated actors' (ibid., p. 176), refers to the more generally used notion of structure, that is patterned behaviour that exists over time. These patterned behaviours are the outcome of a multitude of human actions which by virtue of their sameness have been constituted as structural properties. They do not, and cannot, cause actors to behave in any particular way. Indeed, if Giddens intends to characterise them as forms of constraint, which directly impact upon interactional arenas in which agents make decisions, and if he intends them to operate in the same way as his other two forms of constraint – material impediments and negative sanctions – then he has to show how those patterns of behaviour developed. Halsey (1975, p. 17) makes a similar point:

> A theory which explains educational achievement as the outcome of a set of individual attributes has lost the meaning of those structural forces which we know as class. An adequate theory must also attend to those structural inequalities of resource allocation which are integral to a class society.

In other words, material impediments and negative sanctions are in part responsible for human agents behaving in similar ways, and thus allow patterned behaviours. An example would be gendered relations in schools impacting on and restricting learning programmes for girls. It is the rules and arrangements of resources which operate in particular schools and generally in the school system which constitute the setting; which provide good reasons for actors within those settings to behave in the way they do.

Finally, we need to examine those decision-making arenas in schools. They can be characterised by degrees of formality: staff and departmental meetings, individual face-to-face contacts, teachers reading texts of various sorts on their own. We have already suggested a number of features. First, they are made up of a number of differently resourced agents. Second, organisational arrangements determine that some interactional arenas are more important than others. Third, it is the topic under discussion that influences the degree of impact of any interactional exchange. Fourth, the type (especially with regard to time, place and agenda) of interaction influences outcomes. Fifth, transactions between different parts of education systems (usually, but not always, expressed as policy texts) influence the way a new initiative is received in schools.

State Control

Within this framework, there is scope for the central authority to reassert control in three ways. First, those policy texts which convey messages from one part of the system to another can be rewritten. In extreme cases this could involve legislative action. Thus the text can be changed or amended, so that readers are more or less constrained than they were before. This rewriting may also involve a repositioning if the new text changes the rules by which it is read. Future transactions between the different parts of the system are now carried out from a different base, with some parts acquiring greater leverage and influence and others having less. The textual messages concerning devolution of some funding decisions to schools (local financial management) had the effect of repositioning the financial text as LEA powers in this field declined. The changes to coursework arrangements in the GCSE involved a rewriting of the text, and a repositioning of that amended text, which now has greater relevance to, and bestows greater powers on, examination boards, with consequent diminutions of relevance and powers for teachers.

The second way for the central authority to reassert control is directly through legislative action to change the relationship between the different parts of the system, and thus to redistribute abilities and capabilities to influence events. Deem (1994) discusses the way legislation passed in 1986 (No. 2 Education Act), 1988 (the Education Reform Act) and 1993 (Education Act) has progressively reshaped the composition, duties and, more importantly, powers of school governing bodies. The introduction of a National Curriculum and a national system of assessment (legislated for in the 1988 Education Reform Act) has had, and continues to have, a considerable impact on relationships, and respective spheres of influence, between the different parts of the system.

The third way that the centre can reassert control over the periphery is by changing the arrangements for resource allocations in the system. We have already referred to the context – biographical, material and structural – within which practitioners make decisions and formulate strategies; a context, moreover, that is forever evolving as agents work within it. That context can be changed by decisions made by the central authority, which operate as constraints on action at a local level. In short, teachers operate in terms of these contexts and their powers to devise their own teaching and learning strategies are restricted by them. Evolving arrangements for National Curriculum assessments provide us with a case study of these policy processes.

National Curriculum Assessments

In the context of the introduction of the National Curriculum, four assessment phases can be identified. The first, which found its fullest expression in the TGAT Report (DES, 1988a), emphasised the central place of teacher assessments in pedagogic processes, recommended a system of terminal and summative assessments at the end of each key stage to ensure the comparability and reliability of those teacher assessments, proposed a ten-level system to encourage progression with the average pupil expected to change levels every two years, adopted a criterion-referenced framework so that pupils' achievements were assessed against written statements, was fundamentally opposed to assessments being made which were separate from, and not connected to, curricula, and suggested that results at the end of three of the key stages should be published without being adjusted for the socio-economic background of the individuals and schools concerned. In the second phase, a number of significant changes to the original model were made. These downgraded the importance of teacher assessment, with consequent losses in the ability of teachers to make formative assessments. Henceforth, end-of-key-stage summative assessments were to be the principal method used. Teacher assessments would cover those attainment targets which could not be covered by SATs, and more significantly, be the mechanism by which it was decided at which level of SATs pupils would be entered. The third phase, which coincided with the appointment of a new Secretary of State, was in effect a continuation of the trend established in phase two. Instead of SATs which were long, interactive, had formative potential, and were closely connected to curricula, the development agencies were instructed to deliver 'paper and pencil', summative, easily managed and simpler-to-process end-of-key-stage tests. At the same time coursework components in the GCSE (key stage 4) were statutorily reduced, and the publication of 'raw' tests scores was endorsed by the 1992 Education Act. The 'Dearing' phase separated formative and summative purposes of assessment, repositioned on an equal basis teacher assessments and SATs, questioned the need for a ten-level system and suggested replacing it by four separate reporting stages, and proposed a slimming down of both curricula and assessment.

Phase One – Mixed Messages

The Task Group on Assessment and Testing published its report in 1988 (DES, 1988a), followed by three supplements (DES, 1988b) a few months later. They argued that a fully integrated system of assessment can and should be formative and summative:

Promoting children's learning is the principal aim of school. Assessment lies at the heart of this process. It can provide a framework in which educational objectives may be set and pupils' progress charted and expressed. It can yield a basic platform for planning the next educational steps in response to children's needs. By facilitating dialogue between teachers, it can enhance professional skills and help the school as a whole to strengthen learning across the curriculum and throughout its age range.

(par. 3)

Later changes to the assessment arrangements have concentrated on unpicking this apparent conflation within the same system of these two fundamental purposes (either by downgrading one at the expense of the other, such as in phase three; or clearly separating the different purposes, as Dearing (1993) suggested in phase four). The problem is both conceptual and organisational. Formative and summative (and therefore evaluative) modes of assessment are, it is argued, fundamentally opposed, though the latter can provide useful but limited diagnostic information.

Formative aspects of assessment are most closely associated with the process of teaching itself, but it is the results of summative assessment which are most public and visible. Formative assessment sets out to provide information for the teacher about the way pupils complete particular tasks. The information produced is intended to feed directly into the teaching process, and the focus is therefore on how pupils tackle those tasks and how they proceed with them, as well as what results they achieve. The context in which assessment is undertaken does not need to be standardised for formative purposes, although it may be noted as relevant. From formative assessment, the teacher draws conclusions about how to move the pupils' learning forward, and thus allow plans to be made for the next stage of the teaching.

Summative assessment is concerned with determining whether pupils have mastered particular elements of the curriculum. Summative assessments aim to be reliable and valid, and homogeneity of context is important so that comparability is possible and so that no pupil is disadvantaged. A summative assessment marks some point in the otherwise potentially 'organic' teaching–learning process at which it is decided to stop teaching and give full attention to assessment. The stage at which it is most appropriate and desirable to carry out this kind of assessment is often determined by factors other than those arising from learning goals, such as predetermined times in the school year, or a requirement to report to other interested parties.

TGAT further argued that assessments should be connected (Goldstein, 1989) and not separated from curricula:

The assessment system being proposed differs from most of the standardised testing that is now used in many primary schools and some
secondary schools. Those tests are not related closely to what children
are being taught, and when they identify children likely to have difficulties they give little indication of the nature of problems. Their purpose
is to compare children with each other and with samples of children
with whom the tests were originally developed, often many years ago.

(DES, 1988a, par. 76)

Assessments may be more or less closely integrated with the teaching
programmes which pupils follow. Some kinds of assessment are not actually
designed to measure the pupils' learning (or the results of the teachers'
teaching), in which case they are often associated with measures of qualities
supposedly inherent in the pupil, such as 'intelligence'. Assessment which is
placed at the 'integrated' end of the continuum is likely to be more informal
than formal, more formative than summative, process- as well as product-
orientated, and to be frequent or continuous rather than taking place on
one predetermined occasion at the end of the course.

TGAT advocated a criterion-referenced system of assessment:

. . . in which an award or grade is made on the basis of the quality of
the performance of the pupil, irrespective of the performance of other
pupils, this implies that teachers and pupils be given clear descriptions
of the performances being sought.

(DES, 1988a, par. 76)

Though norm-referenced systems of assessment have become discredited,
criterion-referenced systems are not without their problems. First, it is much
easier to operate with a simple pass–fail mechanism such as a driving test,
than to apply it to complex multi-level systems such as the National
Curriculum. Criteria are relatively easy to identify for the purposes of testing a performance like driving proficiency, but much harder to associate
precisely with the range of levels related to learning as envisaged in the
National Curriculum. Second, criterion-referenced systems conflate logical
hierarchies of skills and content with developmental approaches to learning
employed by pupils. Third, there is a conceptual anomaly, in that the process of establishing criteria appropriate to the various levels involves some
notion of an 'average student' which means that a normative component is
involved.

The fourth element of the assessment scheme proposed by TGAT was the
reporting arrangements. They recommended that there should be no
requirement of a school or LEA to publish information about the results
of the assessments made at key stage one. At other stages they suggested
that 'raw' data should be published, but:

> . . . only if this is done in the context of reports about that school as a whole, so that it can be fair to that school's work and take account so far as possible of socio-economic and other influences.
>
> (DES, 1988a, par. 18)

The arguments against this approach and in favour of 'value-addedness' have been well rehearsed (not least by Dearing, 1993). However, it quickly became policy to publish such information in league or alphabetically arranged tables without reference to the school's socio-economic profile in the form of any general statement.

TGAT thus combined different functions of assessment, incorporated different models of school improvement and supported conflicting notions of accountability. Two models of assessment can be identified. The first of these models argues that information gathered during assessments should be used by teachers and students to plan future learning experiences. Assessment as part of school improvement is perceived as *contextualised* – the timing of the assessments, their relationship to the specifics of the course, and the conditions under which they were undertaken are all taken into account as teachers and pupils interpret the results; *ipsative* – the assessments refer only to the teaching and learning of those pupils and their past achievements, and comparisons with other pupils and schools cannot be drawn from them; and *non-competitive* – this emphasises a professional commitment to high standards of teaching rather than a competitive incentive to outperform other pupils, teachers or schools. More importantly, this model places a low emphasis on external accountability, whether in the context of free-market consumerist or state-control notions of accountability. Accountability may be directly to the pupils, but in the context of professional integrity rather than in response to external pressure.

The alternative model characterises assessment as *decontextualised* – here a high emphasis is placed on comparability, so that variables peculiar to particular pupils, teaching situations or schools are not given the same priority as they are in the first model; and as *competitive* – a teacher's work is judged in relation to the achievements of his or her peers. This model places a high emphasis on external accountability. Indeed in line with Kogan's (1986) free-market consumerist model of accountability, failure in the context of the public market place leads to loss of income for the school and of employment for teachers. Aspects of both models featured in the initial TGAT report, though subsequent arrangements made for assessment of the National Curriculum are more in line with our second model. It is hardly surprising that the TGAT Report was read differently by different people, some pointing to progressive features (Brown, 1992; Lawton, 1992); others identifying more regressive elements (Noss et al., 1989).

Phase Two – Adjustments by the Central Authority

TGAT had made a number of recommendations about the role and importance of teacher assessments. The chief purpose of SATs (end-of-key-stage tests) was to ensure reliability and comparability, and further-more it was suggested that these should work at the class and not individual level. If they diverged, the teacher assessment was to be adjusted. The School Examination and Assessment Council (SEAC, 1989a) proposed in response to the TGAT report that:

> First, teachers would assess pupils on every attainment target . . . sub-ject scores would be aggregated and passed on to local moderators in the spring. Second, teachers would administer SATs in the summer to all pupils 'but possibly only for some attainment targets'. Where avail-able, the SAT result would displace the teacher assessment.

They went further at the end of the year in making the following recom-mendations to the Secretary of State (SEAC, 1989b):

1 By the end of the spring term preceding the end of the key stage there should be recorded teacher-assessment giving the level each pupil had reached in each attainment target.
2 When the SATs have been used in the summer term there will also be a recorded SAT outcome for some attainment targets – probably not all.
3 Where (1) and (2) yield the same outcome for each profile component, that is the end of the matter. The SAT outcome for the attainment, where there is one, should stand.
4 Where (1) and (2) yield a different outcome for any profile component, the SAT outcome may be used for the pupil record if the teacher is con-tent. If the teacher believes (1) should be used, the teacher will be required to make a case for this choice through local moderating arrangements, details of which still await clarification.

These proposals formed part of the final standing orders published in July 1990. They also included complicated rules for aggregating attainment target achievements, and aggregating profile achievements into subject achievements. The new orders signalled a radical change of direction. Henceforth, assessment, moderation and reporting would operate at indi-vidual attainment target level and, more importantly, SATs were to be the main method of assessment, with teacher assessments being marginalised.

Despite this, the Secretary of State at this time, John MacGregor (1990), was still arguing in favour of a number of the principles enshrined in TGAT, namely that assessment should be firmly connected to curricula and that teachers had a central role to play in assessment arrangements:

> The tasks themselves have been designed to be indistinguishable from the kinds of work that most seven year old pupils are used to. . . . Turning to 14 year olds, I have indicated to the School Examinations and Assessment Council that I shall expect the arrangements for assessing technology, history and geography and modern foreign languages – to combine both teacher assessment and statutory standard Assessment Tasks . . . both continuous assessment and end of year examinations are much more generally established in secondary schools, so that the new arrangements should be able to grow that much more readily out of existing practice.

He was referring to the successful implementation of coursework in the GCSE, a move much derided by the New Right (North, 1987; Marenbon, 1987; Beattie, 1987). O'Hear (1987) for instance argued that the then new examination would be less rigorous, would lead to a downgrading of standards and would not allow 'genuine comparisons' between pupils. Worthen (1987, p. 30), likewise, suggested about teacher assessments that 'no man should be a judge in his own cause', reflecting a clear distrust of professional and collegial modes of accountability.

Assessment arrangements in this phase were in a state of transition with no clear ideological line as yet forthcoming. Without recourse to legislation however, significant amendments were being made on a number of fronts. First, the text was being rewritten with the result that teachers would experience significant amounts of disempowerment. It was becoming more 'readerly' and less 'writerly' (Barthes, 1975). Second, the amended text was being repositioned in the system so that relations between the different parts were being reordered. What was also beginning to emerge was a desire by the central authority to re-enforce and augment public or state control modes of accountability. In phase three, the trend became clearer.

Phase Three – Reassertion of Control

In 1990, a new Secretary of State, Kenneth Clarke, took over. He was determined to reassert the power of the central authority over its constituent bodies. He thus wanted to limit and circumscribe the power of the individual teacher, 'the professional expert', by reordering relations between the different parts of the system. He inherited a number of problems: the first SATs appeared to be too long, too detailed and difficult to manage. They also demanded considerable input by teachers with the result that doubts began to be expressed about their reliability and comparability. Furthermore, it was suggested that standards were being eroded in the GCSE, as the number of candidates obtaining high grades increased year by year. The Secretary of State acted in two ways. First, a number of key stage three SAT development contracts were terminated, and new specifications set out. These asked the Mathematics Development Agency, for instance, to produce at key stage three, three one-hour tests covering all the content attainment targets. Process attainment targets were to be assessed by non-statutory SATs, and there was to be a general revision and culling of attainment targets. Brown (1992, p. 17), writing about these new orders, noted that:

> The irony of this decision to revert to short written tests is that they are purported to be in the interest of teachers who, it was assumed – before waiting for evidence to the contrary to become available – would find the KS3 SATs unmanageable and disruptive.

The effect of this type of testing was problematic. First, it limited the ability of the assessments to allow formative and diagnostic judgements to be made. Second, it further separated assessment from curricula by restricting and standardising the way those assessments were to be made (Brown (1992), for instance, estimated that pupils would be allowed six minutes to demonstrate mastery of each statement of attainment). And third, it further downgraded the importance of teacher assessments.

A similar move occurred with the coursework arrangements in the GCSE, the political rhetoric emphasising reliability, comparability and the maintenance of standards. The Secretary of State argued that:

> Coursework should play an important part in its curriculum, but not all of it is good. SEAC and HMI have constantly identified cases in which there is too much variation in the tasks set, too much diversity in marking and moderation, and too much opportunity for cheating. It may not give a true and honest indication of a pupil's ability.
>
> (Clarke, 1991)

From 1994, the maximum amount of coursework allowed has been: English – 40%; mathematics – 20%; science – 30%; technology – 60%; history – 25%; geography – 25%; social sciences – 20%; business studies – 25%; and economics – 20%.

Phase three then represents the clearest expression of what Gipps (1990) calls 'a standards and accountability model'. In particular, this phase saw considerable emphasis placed on the publishing of league and alphabetically arranged tables of performance, with the unit of currency 'raw' and not adjusted. This and other aspects of the testing arrangements led to a boycott by the teachers' unions, with few schools completing the key stage three statutory tests in the summer of 1993, and a significant number of primary and infant schools abandoning key stage one assessments half way through. The ability of the central authority to impose its agenda on schools was being challenged. The response of the government was to commission the *Dearing Report* (1993, pp. 65–66), with the chairman of the newly created School Curriculum and Assessment Authority (SCAA) being asked to answer four key questions:

1 What is the scope for slimming down the curriculum itself?
2 What is the future of the ten-level scale for graduating children's attainments?
3 How can the testing arrangements themselves be simplified?
4 How can central administration of the National Curriculum and testing arrangements be improved?

Phase Four – Compromise

Dearing (1993), in his report, sought to bridge the divide between the competing parties. He proposed a number of significant amendments. First, though he accepted the need to separate teacher assessments from national test results by recommending that they 'should be shown separately in all forms of reporting and in school prospectuses' (ibid., p. 52), he also argued for those teacher assessments to be moderated in terms of statutory end-of-key-stage tests. Depending on the means used, this could result in two sets of similar results being reported side by side. Despite this, Dearing was attempting here to separate formative and diagnostic purposes of assessment from summative and evaluative ones. This was intended to have the effect of reinforcing the importance of teacher assessments, albeit that they would be moderated by SATs.

He further proposed that the prescribed curricular arrangements as expressed in the published orders should be cut back. The time released would allow: the teaching of non-statutory material as defined by SCAA; the teaching of programmes of study which go beyond those laid down in the new orders; the teaching of subjects not included in the National Curriculum; and the reinforcing of mastery of basic skills. Though the time left would still be small in proportion to the time spent on the prescribed curriculum, this would significantly affect the ability of teachers to contribute to curriculum-making, and thus to be responsive to the needs of their pupils.

The third significant suggestion that Dearing made was that the ten-level system should be re-evaluated. Though alternatives – Dearing proposed four separate age-related systems – did not meet all the objections made about the operant system, the intention was clear: to simplify and clarify, and thus to make workable, these assessment arrangements. He cited three major problems with the ten-level system: first, subject knowledge and skills cannot necessarily be organised in linear patterns; second, pupils do not necessarily learn in simple orderly and linear ways; and third, 'it is difficult to devise clear, unambiguous, hierarchical criteria except for simple or clearly defined tasks' (Dearing, 1993, p. 40). Though he made no recommendation, the suggestion in his report was that the ten-level system, integral to TGAT (DES, 1988a), should be either modified or abolished.

Finally, he argued that there was still a need to collect and publish summative data about pupils and schools. He was sympathetic, but not yet convinced, about the need to rework the 'raw' data to allow for socio-economic factors; and he rejected the arguments for carefully devised light sampling to judge the system year by year. He was thus, whilst separating formative and summative functions of assessment, tying closely together summative and evaluative functions and thus aligning any new model within a standards and accountability framework (Gipps, 1990). The report itself has to be understood as only one stage in the continuing development of assessment arrangements in United Kingdom schools. It was, though, further evidence of the tensions between two conflicting models of accountability. The first of these emphasises professional control over curricula, though teachers would be expected to respond to the demands of external review. The second is a variant on the consumerist model described by Kogan (1986), in which market mechanisms are influential and data are gathered to compare school with school. If those data reflect badly on particular schools, then the market exacts a penalty and the school loses pupils and teachers and may even have to close down.[54]

Concluding Remarks

This historical case study[55] of the evolving arrangements made for assessing the National Curriculum illustrates a number of facets of policy processes. First, though the government would seek to impose education policy on schools, it is subject to, and subjects itself to, a number of important limitations or constraints. There are limits as to how prescriptive texts can be made, since even the most 'readerly' text can be selectively read. Again, given the stated purposes of the government, to write curricular and assessment orders which exclude active roles for teachers would be self-defeating. Though control over curricula has been centralised, to remove all discretion from those whose task it is to implement such curricula would render that implementation as inflexible, inefficient and unproductive. Second, governments and government agencies are composed of individuals with different understandings and different conceptions of policy matters. Policy is thus always contested at this level and at other moments and places in the system, though as has been stressed, 'site' influences are not equally important and individuals working at these 'sites' are not equally empowered. Third, individual agents operating in collectivities can exert a significant influence on governments, even if the views they propagate differ radically from those being advocated 'officially'.

But such a view cannot and should not be seen to support pluralist policy models, which seek to suggest that the final outcome of state policy is always an amalgam of, and compromise between, different interests and concerns. Actors in the policy process adopt positions in terms of contexts which are not of their own making, though their activities contribute to new texts and contexts. These position actors unequally and thus differentially allocate resources and roles. Such a view seeks to provide a corrective to both simplistic pluralist *and* state-control models of curriculum change. These manoeuvrings by policy-makers also form the backdrop to the way practitioners construct and reconstruct themselves as professionals. The next chapter examines this in relation to writing biographies and autobiographies.

8   Biography and Auto-biography

Biography and auto-biography are increasingly being seen as important dimensions of social and educational inquiry (cf. Erben, 1998). This is because the individual and their relations with other individuals are essential to an understanding of social life. This is not to prioritise the individual over society but to emphasise the need to preserve individual agency in the face of structural, institutional and systemic accounts of life. The essential building blocks of the biographical method are the text, the narrative, time, multiple perspectives, relationships between the structural and the agential, traditions of thought and inscriptive practices, interpretation and identity. Though biography and auto-biography focus on the individual life, this is not to suggest that other forms of social inquiry are illegitimate and that other data-collection methods are not appropriate in other circumstances. However, it is to suggest that this form of inquiry allows appreciation of the driving force of society – the complex interactional activity of a number of individuals, all seeking to create and recreate themselves in the context of forms of life which are continually undergoing transformation.

I have already suggested that textual analysis is central to the method. If the subject of the inquiry is dead, then the biographer has to resort to a range of sources which are available to him or her in textual form. These may include: auto-biographies, diaries, letters and other forms of writing by the person themselves; historical accounts and other paraphernalia by contemporaries; secondary accounts produced after the life has ended; and oral histories by contemporaries who are still alive which are collected by the biographer and used in various ways. If the person is still alive, then the texts the biographer will work with are: written material produced by the person during their life, accounts by contemporaries, secondary accounts by other biographers, and more fundamentally, personal testaments recorded in the course of extended interviews. This is textual evidence about the life being studied. It is therefore important to understand the nature of textual evidence in order to determine a proper way of using it. In other words, unless an attempt is made to understand what that evidence is, it is impossible to devise appropriate methods which will allow biographers and auto-biographers to inscribe it in their texts.

Texts

There are two questions to be answered. What is a text? And how do we read it? There are three possible answers to these questions. The first of these is that the text provides an unequivocal reading. This may not equate to the intentions of the author. Whether it does or not is immaterial to the type of reading, especially since many texts are multi-authored. This type of reading transcends time, place and author. The interpretation of such a text is unproblematical, since its meaning is embedded in words and relations between words which can only be understood in one way. This universalising of the reading process is given expression by religious fundamentalists who treat the text as sacred. In the field of ethics, Macintyre (1981, p. 206) suggests that: 'When men and women identify what are in fact their partial and particular causes too easily and too completely with the cause of some universal principle, they usually behave worse than they would otherwise do.' Ways of understanding and therefore ways of reading texts are not immersed in particular time-bound societies and cultures, since meaning transcends the mores and inscriptive practices of any one particular culture. This implies also that there is a correct method for reading a text: freed of incorrect or biased ways of deciphering meaning, the reader uncovers its truth. Both textual meaning and ways of reading texts are universal, trans-epistemic activities. It is enough to say at this point that this framework for reading texts leads to certain unanswered questions. We will see later how different cultures through time are immersed in different traditions of thought; that is, they literally understand the world in different ways and inscribe that understanding idiosyncratically. Furthermore, because the texts we are dealing with here, auto-biographical accounts, operate in a dialectical fashion with the construction of the self by the person whose life it is, this adds a further complication.

The second way textual analysis may be understood is in terms of the text being a way of understanding the author's intention. This position is diametrically opposed to the notion of the authorless text. The biographer seeks to reconstruct the life by reading into the text the intentions of the person who constructed it and which preceded it; or, in other words, a pure reading of the text of an extended interview would look beneath the surface, would deconstruct the presentational qualities of the text and uncover a truthful perception of the person's life. The person whose life it is, is not reconstructing that life, but telling it imperfectly. The biographer understands these imperfections and uses the only available evidence, the imperfect presentational account, as a clue to what really happened. There are two implications of this. First, this viewpoint implies that present understandings do not affect past understandings; that we understand what happened in the past in the same way as we did then; in short, that there is a fixed way of interpreting which does not change (or if it does change, this is purely because of error or faulty memory) and that understanding is not culturally and historically located. Second, this viewpoint suggests that inscription or indeed verbal interpretation is only a mask for an underlying truth. If accounts of lives are always merely presentational, then to use the text as a pretext for discovering an underlying meaning – to be equated with authorial intention – is to condemn the interpretation of the life to a sterility which diminishes it.

The third approach is to acknowledge that the text and the way it is read are embedded in history. Heidegger (1962) points to the 'fore-structure' of interpretation and he means by this that 'an interpretation is never a presuppositionless apprehending of something presented to us', but always involves a 'forehaving', 'foresight' and 'foreconception'. Historical texts are therefore read in terms of their pre-texts – each society has its own way of organising language, discourses and writing, and thus any historical text has a form which is unfamiliar to the reader (cf. Usher, 1997). Reading texts is therefore essential to auto/biographical study.

Biographical/Auto-biographical Method

Educational exegesis comprises the study of individuals and collections of individuals living together and immersed in society. Thus biography or biographical study is the sine qua non of understanding how education systems function, of how society is reproduced and constructed through schooling, and of how knowledge of and within such systems is made available. However, biography has to confront two dilemmas. The first of these concerns the relation between auto-biography and biography, and the second, the interrelationship of structure and agency. Biographers come face to face with auto-biographical texts situated in time and place. These auto-biographical texts, collected in the course of extended interviews, are reconstructions by participants of their own fragmented lives and are thus bricolages. They are made coherent by an act of methodological closure agreed between participant and researcher, these closure devices always having a history and conforming to the arrangements made for textual production at particular moments in time. These methodological agreements are, furthermore, negotiated; that is, relations of power enter into these accounts of peoples' lives.

The 'life' is therefore made in terms of the past reconstructed by the participant in the present; that is, past events transformed or retranslated to be narratively coherent, given the epistemological mores of the present. It is never simply enough to understand the process as one of remembering, or of course not remembering (given the frailty of memory), a past life and then representing that account as truthful. It is, as Macintyre (1988) reminds us, that knowledge of the world and the self is always embedded within traditions of understanding which allow us to say some things and do not allow us to say other things, and furthermore, to say some things in some ways and not in other ways. We therefore literally reconstruct the past with reference to how we understand the present.

We have already conceded that this understanding is social. However, unless we want to take a purely phenomenological perspective, which is that participants' accounts of their lives and activities are always adequate, then we need to go beyond this. Bhaskar (1989) for instance, argues that this phenomenological perspective assumes unjustifiably that participants have full knowledge of the perspectives which underpin their everyday actions. In other words, social actors are not able to transcend the limitations of consciousness. This can be expressed in four ways: human beings do not have full knowledge of the settings which structure their activities; human beings cannot have knowledge of the unintended consequences of their actions because the translation of intention to fulfilment of project is never unproblematic, and furthermore, what actually happens is the sum of a multitude of human projects which have unforeseen consequences; third, social actors may not be aware of unconscious forces which drive them towards projects which consciously they do not wish to complete; and fourth, social actors operate with tacit knowledge which they are unable to articulate or are unaware of as they go about their lives.

What are the implications of this for the biographer? The latter is complicit in the production of an account which offers a different perspective on that life, indeed always goes beyond it. This is so for two reasons: the biographer brings with them to the act of research both their own biography, that is, a set of presuppositions about their own life which is of course transitive and presently constituted, *and* knowledge of the process of doing research. In short, they are positioned both in terms of their own biography and in terms of those epistemological frameworks through which they understand the world. For some (cf. Derrida, 1976) the closure occasioned by the researcher constitutes an act of violence; biography as opposed to auto-biography is always violent. However, the violence of this act is never absolute because, as I suggested above, the power of the researcher to impose unequivocally their interpretation on 'the life' is constrained and willingly constrained by how they understand their role. Biographers for example, usually consult and negotiate about the completed account. They may have incomplete knowledge of the way the account is constructed and comes to fruition. Fundamentally though, they may be in sympathy with the project of their participant and thus the types of closure they mediate may be in accord with those of the participant. What is indisputable however, is that the account is constructed by both researcher and participant, and thus conforms to a greater or lesser extent with particular agendas, and that those agendas always make reference to the past – both the past of the biographer and that of the participant. As Erben (1996) notes, this is why the biographical method is frequently referred to as auto/biographical method. The interpretive or hermeneutical procedure implicit in the biographical act is necessarily replicative of the process undertaken by the auto-biographer.

Structure/Agency Dilemmas

We now come to the second dilemma for biographical researchers. Biography is the study of an individual in society or, in other words, it comprises an understanding of the relations between agency and structure with reference to that individual. The most compelling problem then, is the precise relationship between structure and agency, which is of course an ontological matter, and then between this relationship and that of the biographer, which on the surface seems to be purely an epistemological matter. However, the precise epistemological mode becomes an ontological matter since the text produced has real material effects, albeit in discursive form. Social life therefore has a recursive shape or may be characterised by a double hermeneutic (Giddens, 1984). Human beings both generate and are in turn influenced by social scientific descriptions of social processes and this introduces an instability into social research which renders the production of law-like propositions about social activities, and in particular 'the life', as problematic.

In Chapter 3 I sought to show how various theorists have attempted to reconcile the phenomenological and the structural. Four possible solutions were identified: downwards conflation, upwards conflation, central conflation or structuration and morphogenesis. Since downwards conflation prioritised structure over agency and upwards conflation prioritised agency over structure, both were felt to be inadequate to the task of providing a proper explanation of the relationship between the two. Morphogenesis was deemed to offer a more appropriate conceptualisation of this relationship because structuration was seen to have tied them too closely together. The important point is that any theory has to avoid reification, especially of structural properties, and at the same time acknowledge the dialectical nature of the relationship which exists between self and society. Furthermore, actors' accounts of the transformation of the self over time and of those structural properties which were implicit in the process have also to be understood in the context of the biographical method.

Social actors' accounts of their agency at particular moments of time are retrospective and delivered in terms of different contexts from which they were originally enacted. The social actor offers an account which has a wave-like form. Past events are construed at different moments in life and then reconstructed again and again in different circumstances. However, it is not the original event which is subsequently reconstructed but the previous reconstruction. Furthermore, as we noted above, the reconstruction which takes place has both a form and a content. Usher (1997, p. 36) suggests a number of important ways of understanding this. Each text has a context 'in the sense of that which is with the text. What is "with" the text in this sense is the situated auto-biography of the researcher/reader'. Reference has already been made to this by locating the auto-biographical text within biography and by suggesting that each text has a pre-text, a form which is essentially social: 'research texts have a pre-text in the sense of that which is before the text; language as the repository of meaning, discourses as particular ways of organising meanings, the textual strategies, literary conventions and rhetorical devices of writing' (Usher, 1997, p. 37). Additionally, each text has a sub-text and an inter-text. The sub-text refers to the epistemological frameworks which constitute particular arrangements of power in history and which have definite effects. Intertextuality may be characterised by: 'the structure of the trace . . . the interlacings and resonances with other traces' (Wood, 1990, p. 47).

Thus each reconceptualisation of a past event has a context, pre-text, sub-text and is implicated with other texts. For the biographer each text has a recursive element, a bending-back on itself, even if it is always presently constituted. The 'life' is a text constituted in and through history. Social actors make sense of their lives in terms of particular discursive arrangements – how events are understood at particular moments of time. These public events are subsequently understood in different ways. Since they were originally ideological in nature, they are contested not least at the political/policy level, and this changes through time and with it the nature of its embeddedment. The social context is literally transformed before the eyes of participants. The social actor therefore has a number of choices, and these choices refer to how they reconstruct public events auto-biographically. They can attempt to conform to how these events are presently understood; they therefore make a conscious decision to renounce their past understanding as inadequate and to view past events in a different way; or they adapt their understanding so that different historical and ideological agendas are reconciled – this of course produces a minimum of dislocation and confusion; or they can be resolute in their beliefs, utterly non-conformist, and understand their life in terms of a relatively intransitive agenda. How they understand the mechanism of the production and reproduction of their 'life' determines its nature.

And for Ricoeur (1984, 1985, 1986) this always occurs within narrative forms. The narrative (or narratives) gives meaning to the expression of self by the social actor; and these narratives are truly social and therefore embedded in time. The central figure in this biographical account is a secondary school teacher in the London Borough of Brent. The narratives which structure it all involve resolution of the personal and the social, and can therefore be said to be dialectical. They comprise three stories: the first is about the child becoming adult; the second is about migration and nationality; and the third is about incorporating public discourses into personal projects. Narrativity therefore allows, as Erben (1996, p. 164) suggests: 'the individual life to emerge in the dual nature, first, of its distinctiveness (person "X" can never be person "Y") and, second, its connectedness (person "X" can "recognise" the narrative of person "Y")'.

A Teacher's Life

Mary O'Brien[56] was brought up in Ireland in the 1950s and 1960s in a semi-rural environment, characterised by migration and the idea of betterment through education:

> And I come from an area where, in the fifties and sixties, there was mass emigration and very, very little by way of industry, some fishermen, small farmers, subsistence farming and very few professions in that area, and yet in my generation and the previous generation, the number of professionals that came out of the small National School was absolutely fantastic.

Furthermore, the 'education' was valued not just as a means of gaining material rewards or pursuing a career but for its own sake:

> There was a great deal of interest in education and, in parts of Ireland, we still have a pretty peculiar vocabulary for instance with people who go to school we called 'scholars' as in Shakespeare day, but at least they were using the word 'scholar'.

The educational was understood as a form of self-revelation. However, the narrative which dominated life in rural Ireland at this time was movement or migration – the desire to uproot, explore and even escape from present circumstances:

> Emigration really characterised the experience of the people, there was quite a haemorrhage of the people from Ireland in the fifties.

As we will see, Mary was to follow this path. However, this did not involve a dissolution of the past, but a reconceptualisation of it in terms of different images, discourses, narratives and contexts. Her Catholic upbringing remains an important defining influence:

> The Catholic ethos . . . was also tied up with our interest in the historical and cultural past. The Catholic ethos would have been defined in

terms of perhaps being a good citizen . . . and also it was a very strong moral outlook in terms of family values and being able to meet responsibilities and also an acceptance of what life might dish out to you. There was within the school that I went to a very strong emphasis on developing potential and there wasn't a ceiling a person might aspire to and not a lot of discussion about the limitations that might affect girls' futures.

Aspirations were nurtured, boundaries dissolved, achievement emphasised, but always within a liberal Catholic framework which stressed the intrinsicality of personal growth and public service:

I think the emphasis for us in terms of careers would have been very much based on the caring professions . . . I am sure that has deeply affected me in my subsequent career, and I am sure that in terms of occupations which are more geared to the world of finance and business then I am sure that my antipathy or my lack of interest in those professions is very much, has been very much engendered by the teaching I experienced in those schools.

Furthermore, that sense of burgeoning identity, framed within a Catholic ethos, was also specifically Irish, in that it furnished her with a set of literary resources that were to prove seminal:

I see my identity in terms of my appreciation of the tradition that I am rooted in. That, I think, now gives me a great deal of comfort and it allows me to grow with inner reserves and in all sorts of ways and I very much appreciate the fact that I have been able to learn the language. I am bi-lingual. I have a good knowledge of Irish history and literature and it gives me a security to perhaps tap in to other cultures and other literatures, especially in terms of teaching in the inner city, that is as an English teacher in an inner city school. It perhaps has also given me that impetus to ensure that writers from, as they say in the exam boards, from other cultures, the Naipauls and the Walcotts, that they actually feature on the diet that is offered to the students in the English classes and that confidence, that diversity and quality, you know, is for the better.

This repudiation of insularity has found expression in her use of sources and resources for teaching from a wide variety of environments.

In addition, the experience of being Irish and colonised engendered a sense of identification with oppressed minority groups and has been an important influence on her perspective, beliefs and notions about education.

Once again we see how events in the past have been reconceptualised as present discourses and influence public stances at different moments in life:

> So there was that feeling of perhaps of injustice which was very conditioned by my own experience in the Irish system. I think my understanding was further engendered by the notion that we had to succeed in the educational system largely on account of our inferior past, that the draining of the economy which we were led to believe, as students, owed a lot to our colonization, that my attitude to education was very much conditioned by my understanding of colonization and so it was relatively easy for me to relate the experiences of Irish people in the education system to those from other colonized areas.

This sense of injustice is reinforced by personal experiences, the more compelling because they were unexpected. She had expected to find that professional teachers would be committed to anti-racist and anti-discriminatory policies and that they would be sophisticated enough not to indulge in crude racism and discrimination:

> I was aware as a young teacher that the sort of anti-Irish feeling that I would have been aware of in a detached way, perhaps in an academic way, I was actually shocked when they began to impinge on me as a professional in a London school and I was acutely aware of it on two occasions; one when a teacher referring to Marilyn was offering some creative excuse for being late and this tutor turned to me, this was my first day of teaching which will give you some idea, this tutor turned to me and said 'How Irish of her,' and I was scandalised, not really from a racist front, but in a snobbish sort of way. I expected this teacher to be able to articulate in a different mode and I remember being taken aback at the quality of her expression.

Personal experiences, remembered and then reconceptualised at different moments in life, provide compelling reasons for action.

Furthermore, her notions of how professionals should behave, nurtured by her experiences in the Irish educational system, were such that she was surprised at the low levels of professional behaviour which she found. Again the image of succour or nurture is foremost and this is contrasted with a relative lack of care given to trainee teachers and with how they subsequently behaved:

> In terms of Irish professionals within the education system, I think the point I would want to make is that because of the economic situation the teacher training colleges and, perhaps, the universities could demand a very high level of entry and therefore I equated that context

with the English system and when I moved from perhaps a selective, for it was a selective system, that I knew in Ireland to the comprehensive system in England, I was expecting to find perhaps colleagues who had perhaps been through a very rigorous education system. I did not find that it was a very general characteristic although clearly there were pockets of it, very definite pockets of it, and so I suppose I was disappointed to find myself as a new teacher in a system where perhaps teachers were not nurtured or perhaps the quality of training given to teachers was not on a level that I might have expected from the selective system in Ireland.

This found its most vivid expression in the low levels of their commitment to the children. Paradoxically, within a selective Irish educational system the ethos she experienced was inclusive; whereas in an English comprehensive system her initial impression was that it was exclusive, in particular with regards to working-class and black children:

But I was mindful that working class kids were just not given the sort of opportunities that working class kids in Ireland had been given and these were kids who were further disadvantaged by being black kids.

Her idea of professionalism also comprised two further notions: first, that the community would award high status to teachers; and second, that reward had attached to it a corresponding obligation of best performance from the teachers themselves. The conjoining here of reward with public duty is echoed elsewhere in this account:

Yes, the teacher would have respect, perhaps not status as an accountant might have status or be a member of the golf course or attend, you know, these sorts of social functions that others in the community might, but in terms of the sort of respect that was afforded to priests, there was some of that respect was given to school teachers, definitely, and the antipathy that the bad teacher in fact would have been afforded.

Social pressures were brought to bear on those teachers who failed to live up to the standards expected of professional people.

This discrepancy between her professional values and her experiences teaching in an English comprehensive school was given expression by the need to resolve the crisis she felt when she first started teaching in England. The resolution was achieved by personal endeavour and the learning of coping strategies and also more importantly by making use of supportive agencies:

Funnily the worst point in my teaching career was my first couple of years teaching at a school in an inner city, and the problem there was just the lack of transparency, just the total, the indifference that I felt that was given to teaching and learning. It was perhaps the contrast between the very different systems in Ireland and England.

These outside influences comprised the advisory service from the Borough in which she worked. Its officers became an important influence not just because they provided strategies and techniques for overcoming the crisis she felt in her classroom management, but also because she was able to sublimate her personal vision, nurtured in Ireland, into a public vision of education as it was espoused by the Borough in which she worked:

But I am positive that the drive for comprehensive schools in the early seventies was only augmented due to the efforts of very competent advisors who had the vision, who had strategies for developing the techniques and the resources that teachers could develop in the classroom and I am very mindful of that, but the system as a whole has not delivered.

This resolution of earlier difficulties in the classroom left its mark. Her present success has to be understood in terms of how she now understands her past, both cognitively and affectively:

I think that I've striven for those standards on account of those early experiences when I was so frustrated, and now find classroom management very, very interesting when I work on it. I find teaching in a class absolutely stimulating, even after twenty five years and I am convinced that it's not just, you know, a natural development, I'm convinced that I am still harping back to the days when I could not do it and that it is almost a relief when I can.

The important point here is that she is dealing with a notion of the past self as it is understood in the present and the reconciliation that is achieved is a reconciliation of remembered experiences.

Her vision of education was and is public and political: a fair and just society can in part be achieved by the work of the education service. What happens in classrooms has a profound effect on society in general. Teachers therefore have a responsibility to nurture the best instincts of the next generation, and teaching can therefore never be just another form of employment:

I think that what I was unconscious of, when I stand in front of a class I am still conscious of, or perhaps sub-conscious more than conscious, is that it matters what is happening here in this classroom. It does matter and that the sum total of these learning experiences in the classroom will matter and the pupils need to know that as well.

This stress on providing beneficial experiences for children in schools leads her to express it in terms of managing learning experiences, which on the one hand taps into current discourses about education; but on the other, allows her to feed into a discourse of empowerment:

I think that the emphasis on management and the opportunities for teachers to tap into knowledge and ways in which good management works, I think that that has to be an enormous advance. We were very much speaking the language of more effective management, there is no doubt about that.

Again, there is an attempt to reconcile past and present understandings. Empowerment remains for her the dominant motif of her professional life, given expression as it was by influential public bodies, in this case the advisory service which had a responsibility for the school in which she worked. These influential sources were to be neutralised by policy enactments and legislation in the 1980s, but while they existed, they were enormously influential and empowering:

We were, as young mid scale teachers, we were very conscious that in the late seventies and early eighties we felt empowered and we also were mindful, perhaps, of the sort of experiences that we had as young teachers in classrooms where black kids were not able to attain much. We were drawing on our immediate experience and this was, finally, a way in which we could see opportunities for black kids you see and we were the ones, and I talk about this in the grass roots movement, pretty much empowered by leading advisors in the Borough and also tapping in to elected members and to community groups and to other sources of academic research, so it was quite a developed movement.

However, this discourse of empowerment which, though led by the Local Education Authority, was essentially a grass roots movement also tapped into current discourses about effective schools. The notion of effectiveness, however, is understood as inclusive and it comprises a particular responsibility to low achievers and the economically disadvantaged:

On the basis that the management structures were not functioning and that management was not taking consideration of their responsibilities and so we were very mindful of management roles and responsibilities . . .

So these were the avenues which enabled us then to look at perhaps what constitutes, or what constituted, effective schools because, you know, we were very clear in our hearts that kids were not attaining largely because of the inefficiency of schools.

She incorporates the past into current discourses of education:

But in those days, preequality days, there wasn't much, to my mind, much emphasis on good schools either, or what constituted good schools.

And this resulted in a neglect of those things which mattered to her. However, there is a feeling of loss, a reverting back to a vision of education nurtured by her experiences in the past. Those least able to cope would be neglected:

The focus, what I'm emphasising here, that those people who were part of that, you know, race or gender culture movement of the mid seventies and eighties, that a lot of what they were focusing on was what constituted things interestingly, that is now what has moved forward, but perhaps in a different direction, in some ways a different direction of what we understood things might be, and the emphasis on race and general equality has been lost.

There is also a sense of regret that her professional ethos has been subverted by new arrangements for teachers. As we have seen, notions of professionals engaging with each other to provide good practice in schools is, as she sees it, largely a thing of the past. What it did was to engender a feeling of empowerment, a belief that professional activity could have an impact on public life and that national policy could be responsive to those grass roots practitioners who provided the service:

There was a feeling at the time that, as professionals, we needed to network outside our own immediate profession, and there was a real sense of that taking place . . . That actually was a fact. And any number of conferences, mostly conferences, would suggest that, you know, the real networking had taken place but there was also, going back to the theme of being empowered, there was also the idea that, perhaps, we could impact on national policy.

She was quickly disillusioned of this conceit. Her defence of past activities by her and her fellow professional teachers in Brent is unequivocal, coupled with a sense of regret:

It has made a difference because what I have been talking about is ways which show our adherence to an antiracist approach. We were convinced by it because to us it equated with good education, so basically in this area in Brent you would find, you know, many thriving examples of good education so the kids who have come through the system have entered the work force as, you know, on a level playing field, so at that minimum level we succeeded.

Indeed, for her, the present drive to make schools more effective can be reconciled with past emphases on race and gender equality, even though the rhetoric of Conservative policy reforms of the 1980s and early 1990s comprised concerted attacks on anti-racist and anti-sexist initiatives:

It's not something that we can quantify in some cases, but perhaps, in 1997, more failing schools would have been on the hit list about to be closed down in the Borough of Brent, if we hadn't had that tradition and I would suggest, yes, that there was no reason why Brent, given, you know, the number of variables that characterised the traditions in which failing schools exist, that the fact that there is an absence really, there is no secondary school in Brent on that failure list.

And this is a source of professional pride. Teachers in England and Wales had to confront a series of educational reforms in the late 1980s and early 1990s which changed both their practice and their sense of professionalism. In some ways, these new discourses were disempowering, both because of what they were and because of the speed of implementation. Mary, in common with other teachers, had to make sense of a set of reforms which did not fit, at least on the surface, with her long-held beliefs about educational processes. Though she voiced opposition to them through her professional association, this, she felt, had little effect:

We were so concerned with coming to terms with the reforms and changes, trying to make sense of it and trying to see how our practice could accommodate it that we were overwhelmed, and though we voiced resistance to the negative impacts of it, we were as English teachers able to voice our opposition to the stance etc. but in common with many practitioners I was just taken over by the tide of change.

The failure to oppose effectively these reforms was exacerbated by the dissolution of the local authority power-base which as we have seen provided her with much support in the early years of her career. Interestingly, that same sense of professional pride which characterises her practice was now being brought into play to implement the new reforms:

But, of course, National Curriculum also corresponded, you know, with LM and with the local management, so with a lot more powers being vested in heads, the people who, perhaps traditionally, looked to the LEA and other sources for backing, and moral support and real support, and could no longer rely on that sort of area of expertise and so that would have been an added reason for the acquiescence. Admittedly classroom practitioners, you know, have only so much time on their hands, so by the time they have assimilated the new ideas into their practice, there wouldn't have been much time left over . . . and of course there would have been the professional pride of coming to terms with all the nuances of the National Curriculum, so by the time you have conducted that . . . because of the sheer force of the innovation and the overall attention to detail that was necessary, that just in terms of time that would be left over there wasn't much, and at the same time, because of local management, there were no longer the opportunities to attend courses and specialists outside of the school, you remember staff development . . . Much, much more insular.

Furthermore, the competitive nature of the reforms undermined any real attempts to resurrect past arrangements and necessitated the need to reconceptualise her idea of what it means to be a professional:

And a little later on, not very much later on, we were so mindful of the competitive nature of the market place, so colleagues that we would have quite happily shared experiences and the resources with, colleagues that we would have networked with – that source, you know, our power base or whatever – but they were no longer our natural allies as they were in the early days. Nowadays, it is all about competing and we all have to be concerned about the school's image, and there are very, very crude marketing ploys that we have to implement, very crude.

These are fragments of a life, continually being remade.

Concluding Remarks

They are, moreover, fragments of a particular life as it is presently understood. As we have seen, this text is constructed in terms of four notions: 1) The interpretative process involves an interweaving of two different agendas: those of the person and their biographer; or as Gadamer (1975) puts it a 'fusion of horizons'. By this he meant that we cannot step outside ourselves even for a moment. We are always immersed in our perspectives and frameworks, so that the act of research constitutes a joint act of exploring these positionings. As Usher (1996, p. 22) suggests: 'A fusion of horizons is the outcome of intersubjective agreement where different and conflicting interpretations are harmonised. By comparing and contrasting various interpretations, a consensus can be achieved despite differences – indeed because of differences. Hermeneutic understanding is therefore a learning experience involving "dialogue" between ourselves as researchers and that which we are trying to understand.' This means that any auto-biographical text has to be understood in terms of the context of its construction and this includes the situated auto-biography of the researcher. 2) The past is organised in terms of the present; that is, present discourses, narratives and texts constitute the backdrop to any exploration of the past. It is not that a biography refers to actual events which are then imperfectly recollected, but that past events are interpretations undertaken by the person whose 'life' it is, and that these interpretations always have a pre-text. Furthermore, this pre-text, comprising as it does the means by which meanings are organised in the present, always makes reference to other pre-texts in the past and indeed supersedes them. Wood (1990) refers to these resonances as traces; that which the past leaves to the present. 3) The public and the private can never be disentangled. For the biographer, it is the way the social actor interacts with the structures of society and the way this contributes to their continuation or modification that is of interest. Private acts are therefore also public acts. 4) The 'life' is always fragmentary, comprising parts as opposed to wholes, narratives that never quite come to fruition, disconnected traces, sudden endings and new beginnings. What gives it its meaning is the act of methodological closure agreed between the person and her biographer.

However, the depiction of the 'life' as fragmented and the agreement reached with the participant about it do not take away the responsibility of the author for producing an interpretation. It therefore follows that this account is one of many that could have been made. Indeed, the closure occasioned by the researcher necessarily treats the evidence as fixed and reliable and glosses over ambivalence and uncertainty. This is a 'privileged' reading of the 'life'. Perhaps, as Stronach and MacLure (1997, p. 49) argue, 'the problem is not what will count as an authentic portrait, but the assumptions we make about personhood. We think of the problem as one of representation (the person as given, the portrait as problematic) and we struggle with forms of ethics, social interaction, data analysis and reporting that will "express" the person, squeeze his (sic) essence from the body of data.' They go on to suggest that the problem is how we actually conceptualise the 'life': 'making problematic what we mean by a person' (ibid.). Throughout the account above, I have had to continually confront this dilemma; that is, the use of narrative devices, tropes, metaphors and other rhetorical forms to sustain the integrity of the person to whom I am referring. Even though the commentary is brief and rarely goes beyond the data, it is there to make sense of those data – to provide the reader with the means to recognise that person as a person. In doing this, it is doing no more than that person would do anyway and again here we see the close alignment of auto-biography with biography. The biographer however, stands apart. They cannot own the account in the way that the auto-biographer can. They always impose a view, follow a particular direction, make sense of an event in one way rather than another. They are therefore complicit in the account and have to take responsibility for it. This, as I have suggested, refers to both its content and its form; indeed, the notion of a biographical account is part of that imposed structure. And yet, the solution to this problem is not easy to find. Stronach and MacLure (1997, p. 57) argue that: 'One goal must be to produce accounts which deny the reader that comfort of a shared ground with the author, foreground ambivalence and undermine the authority of their own assertions.' How we do this and whether we do it successfully or not are key elements in the construction of any 'life', let alone that of Mary O'Brien. One of the key social frameworks within which she was positioned and within which she positioned herself was race. The next chapter examines this issue and in particular how we can research it in educational settings.

9 Researching 'Race' and 'Ethnicity'

Debates about the extent and type of school racism have been prominent in educational research.[57] The substance of the disagreement concerns the question of whether or not schools are places which systematically deny equal treatment to ethnic minority children. It is complicated by different definitions of racial discrimination as it is practised in schools, and by different methodological debates about how it is possible to know whether teachers and schools racially discriminate. These are two separate issues, though they are connected. If we operate with a limited definition of what constitutes racial discrimination in schools, ie. that we can only conclude that it has occurred if evidence for it comprises direct discursive data given to the researcher or direct observational evidence collected by the researcher to the effect that the teacher or teachers in the school under investigation are implementing policies and practices which discriminate, then it is relatively easy to settle the dispute one way or the other. However, if our definition of what constitutes racial discrimination in schools is a different one, ie. teachers and schools may not intend their practices to be discriminatory but this is what results, then what constitutes evidence for discrimination is certainly more difficult to collect and may involve inference from indirect evidence. Definitions therefore play an important part in the designation of methodological strategies for determining whether schools and teachers discriminate. There are a number of possible definitions, and which one the researcher adopts determines the type of data collection strategy they implement.

The first of these is the definition used by Foster (1990a, p. 5): 'Practices which restrict the chances of success of individuals from a particular racial or ethnic group, and which are based on, or legitimised by, some form of belief that this racial or ethnic group is inherently morally, culturally or intellectually inferior.' This is a limited definition in the sense that the evidence required to prove or disprove it comprises testimony by those who are practising it that they operate in this way because of certain specified beliefs. What this definition does do is discount practices which the practitioner is unaware of. Thus institutional or systemic forms of discrimination cannot count as examples; indeed, what this definition also rules out is evidence from those who are being discriminated against, on the grounds that they may be mistaken. What seems to them to be discrimination on the basis of the colour of their skin is in fact motivated by other considerations, ie. a desire to correct poor behaviour, life-style incompatibility or whatever.

Adopting strategies for determining whether discrimination, under this definition, occurs or not is further complicated by the difficulty of ever successfully probing the belief systems of those teachers, in the sense that even if they hold racist beliefs, they are unlikely to reveal them to the researcher because they are aware that the researcher will be antagonistic to their beliefs. Their interview data are therefore almost certainly presentational. On the other hand, the researcher may be able to gather compelling evidence from other sources. For example:

> It was one day we came in from games, and we were all wet. In the West Indian Community, growing up as a West Indian it's cultural to braid your hair. Now, a couple of the girls in the class came in and their hair was wet, and with our texture of hair, if it's out and it gets wet it goes frizzy, and it frizzes to the extent that it looks as though it's shrunk. So to prevent that happening the girls were just braiding their hair to keep it stretched. Now a couple of girls were doing that and the teacher walked in while this was going on and she said, 'Oh, you'd better stop that now. You're not in the jungle now'. We were angry. We were upset. But we weren't articulate enough to be able to say anything back to her, to turn the insult round. But we explained why we were doing this, and we said that braiding actually stretches the hair or even pressing can stretch the hair. Pressing is when you use a hot comb and just comb it through your hair. She didn't realise that or she chose not to understand that point, and she said, 'Oh, how do you press your hair then, do you put your head on an ironing board, and get the iron and run it up'. That was what she said and you could see that she didn't have a clue. She was either deliberately trying to wind us up or she really didn't have a clue about our culture or anything about us, and this was the sort of person who was teaching us.
> (Scott, 1990, pp. 42–43)[58]

Evidence of this type may allow the researcher to conclude that this teacher was motivated by racial prejudice, though they still have to ask themselves two questions: Is this an accurate representation of what happened? Do the words used by the teacher indicate that they are racially biased? Evidence of this sort is rarely available for the reasons given above and, furthermore, if this type of evidence was the only evidence available, it would be difficult to conclude that teachers in general were racist.

A second definition could take the following form. Practices are deemed to be racist even if they do not, as it happens, discriminate against individuals from a particular racial or ethnic minority group, but are intended to have these effects because the teacher holds that members of certain racial or ethnic groups are morally inferior. Again, as with our first definition, the researcher is unlikely to be able to gather direct evidence of this, even if the teacher is motivated in this way. Further, it is difficult to believe that a teacher who was explicitly racist and who was determined to discriminate would not in fact have some effect on the life chances of the individuals concerned.

A third definition would include a notion of unintended consequences. Practices would be considered to be racist if they discriminate against individuals from a particular racial or ethnic group, but they do not have to be based on conscious or explicit beliefs that one group is inferior to another. This is a more complicated definition and involves the researcher in data collection activities which focus on whole-school practices. If we unpick this definition, we are left with two possibilities. First, the teacher is not aware of hidden and unconscious biases they hold against members of racial or ethic minority groups and could not reveal them in the course of an interview because knowledge of them is tacit. Indeed, what may characterise the testimony of this teacher would be an explicit rejection of any belief that members of ethnic minority groups were inferior; they may even aggressively advocate non-discriminatory policies and practices. The researcher, in confronting this dilemma, may chose to infer from the teacher's actions that they do in fact hold certain racist beliefs and at the same time that they genuinely do not know what motivates them. The researcher in effect conducts a psychological investigation of the teacher's motives by examining the available evidence collected from observations about how they behave, and draws the appropriate conclusions from it. This is likely to produce conclusions which would certainly be disputed by the teacher him/herself and are also likely to be disputed by the research community at large.

A second explanation would discount unconscious motivations, but would focus on unintended consequences of actions.[59] These occur because social actors may be unaware of the way institutions and systems are structured and thus what is intended has consequences, both now and in the future, which could not have been anticipated. Or they may be unintended because social actors do not have sufficient self-knowledge or knowledge of structural properties to be able to make a considered and reasonable evaluation of the effects of their actions. Or again, there may be unintended consequences because it is impossible to predict what the future holds and what arrangements may exist then, so that it is impossible to make a reasonable judgement about intended actions.[60]

What is at issue here is the amount and type of knowledge held by social actors. There are four different types:

- Ignorance of motivations for action and ignorance of structural constraints and possibilities.
- Ignorance of structural constraints and possibilities but knowledge of personal motivations and intentions.
- Knowledge of structural constraints and possibilities but ignorance of personal motivations and intentions.
- Knowledge of structural constraints and possibilities and knowledge of personal motivations and intentions.

None of these typifications imply perfect knowledge, but only knowledge which is relative to other social actors. In other words, these are ideal characterisations and should not be construed as representing specific individuals or teachers in schools. However, what this typology does do is to allow us to identify the different dimensions of the knowing self, and what is significant is that the researcher cannot anticipate that all the social actors involved operate with the same degree and type of knowledgeability.

What is also being suggested is that teachers in schools are relatively ignorant (to different degrees) about the unintended consequences of their actions. It is pertinent at this point to suggest a number of examples. The curriculum could be structured in a covert racist way. So, for example, history may be taught from a specifically ideological perspective, which acts to perpetuate racist myths:

> At school I was often angry about history and about British Colonialism and the way we were portrayed. It made us out to be weak, childlike, without dignity and stupid.
>
> (Scott, 1990, p. 44)

or,

> Black people have invented all sorts of things that you don't read about in history books.
>
> (Scott, 1990, p. 45)

Weiner (1990) suggests that the United Kingdom National Curriculum history syllabus is insular, chauvinistic and racially biased. It is both what is taught and what is not taught and the way what is taught is realised that constitutes discriminatory behaviour, albeit unplanned by the teacher concerned. Or the pedagogy itself is explicitly racist, again either through neglect, distortion or ideological bias. For example, curriculum materials have in the past only included pictures and diagrams of white children and neglected children of other colours. If we examine wider curriculum issues, we may want to conclude that the mechanism works by excluding:

> It was only as you grow older, you thought, well, you know we don't have black physics teachers and maths teachers. There was racism in the school and it was from the staff, though I doubt if they were ever aware of it.
>
> (Scott, 1991, p. 46)

Some of these practices operate at the level of the classroom, others operate at the level of the institution.

A fourth definition would therefore refer to institutional arrangements if these restrict the chances of individuals from a particular racial or ethnic group and which are enacted by teachers who do not believe that one ethnic group is superior to another, but who are not able to anticipate the consequences of their actions. This allows for the possibility of racialised practices operating in parts as opposed to the whole system. In other words, discrimination is practised locally and is not a function of systemic arrangements. We therefore have to incorporate into this definition a dimension of scope.

Scope refers to whether racial discrimination is conducted by a few isolated individuals acting alone scattered throughout the education system or whether racial discrimination is endemic to all schools by virtue of the way that they are organised which compels teachers to discriminate, whether they know they are doing so or not. This form of institutional discrimination is not unimaginable, especially if we consider the discriminatory element deliberately built into examinations (that is, they discriminate against those students who do not perform[61] well and are underpinned by a notion of different abilities). In terms of scope, it is possible to plot a range of practices:

- Individual and isolated cases.
- A large number of cases.
- All teachers and thus all cases.
- Institutional arrangements which allow teachers to resist them.
- Institutional arrangements which are compelling.[62]

In order to give examples of these last two categories, we would have to identify certain specific behaviours and practices, both discursive and non-discursive, as racist or as having racist consequences. Written documentation which required teachers to treat certain types of students in a different way because of the colour of their skin, ie. that they should be educated in separate schools as in apartheid South Africa, would be an example. This is a relatively straightforward case. However, there are a series of cases documented in the literature which are not as clear cut.

Gillborn (1998) identifies one such controversy. Data have been collected which show that a disproportionate number of children from ethnic minority groups are placed in lower streams. For Gillborn, this constitutes evidence that certain racial and ethnic minority groups are being discriminated against. However, Foster (1990a, p. 96) disagrees:

> If, for example, different cultural norms result in students from a certain group being more noisy, aggressive, inattentive, prone to classroom disruption, or disrespectful of others, then teachers surely cannot, and should not, be expected to accept such behaviour just because it is the product of different cultural norms. I think there is a possibility that this may be the case with some of the cultural norms of certain Afro/Caribbean students – especially those associated with male, youth, subcultural forms.

Foster is arguing that what seems to be an instance of discrimination is merely behavioural incompatibility. African/Caribbean children are under-represented in higher streams because they do not in general behave in the appropriate way. The first point that needs to be made is that Gillborn's focus is misdirected. It is not perhaps the placing of a disproportionate number of African/Caribbean children in lower streams which provides evidence of discrimination but the initial stereotyping that occurred prior to the act of streaming. However, it is more complicated than this, because the act of stereotyping is both cause and consequence of discrimination. Many previous cycles of streaming and stereotyping stretching back in time constitute the conditions which position teachers and students in particular ways. Of course, these structural properties compel no one. However, they do provide the essential conditions for action in the present. The behaviour of African/Caribbean children is in part constructed by arrangements made within each school and certainly, though in a different way, by systemic arrangements. Breaking the cycle requires therefore, both institutional and discursive reform. Foster equally, is misguided, first because he fails to indicate that generalisations made about children by teachers simplify and distort what is in effect a complex matter – the cultural identification of the child – and second because he fails to bring to the attention of the reader that the cultural stereotyping which he makes reference to both describes and serves to construct the child in a stereotypical way. Stereotyping refers to the past and at the same time acts as a structural property and thus has an effect on the present, because the types of structural properties in existence at any one time determine the types and degrees of rewards and sanctions which are the essential conditions for any action.

A full explanation such as this allows us to construct an appropriate methodological strategy. The first part of the strategy comprises the discovery of real mechanisms, which may or may not have been actualised, but which have the potential to lead to discrimination of ethnic minority groups. The second strategy is to show how those mechanisms have worked in practice. This does not mean that they will always work in this way, but what it does do is to allow the researcher to develop an explanation for the persistent pattern of discrimination which has been observed. Racism, in other words, is implicit in the relations between social actors in institutions such as schools. It is covert and would not be admitted to by the key social actors, ie. teachers, but is embedded in the types of practices carried on in the school. In order to sustain this argument, a possible relationship would need to be established between the norms or rules which characterise the life of the school and processes of hierarchisation. Because schools are hierarchical places and because they deliberately set out to induct children into a hierarchically stratified world, then it is only a small step to that hierarchisation taking on a racialised form. Pawson and Tilley (1997, p. 68) define a mechanism as 'not a variable, but an account of the make-up, behaviour and interrelationships of those processes which are responsible for the regularity' which has been observed. 'A mechanism is thus a theory – a theory which spells out the potential of human resources and reasoning' (ibid.). In the case of race, this mechanism may be institutional – and if it is we then have to spell out how institutions are constructed so that if the mechanism is actualised, racial discrimination occurs; or discursive – again we have to understand the structure of the discourse.

Institutional and discursive structures refer to both primary institutions (systems or more particularly educational systems) and secondary institutions (schools, colleges, etc.). There are a number of possibilities. The first of these can be quickly ruled out, which is that institutional policy as it is expressed in various school documents is explicitly racist, and what this means is that there is within these policy documents explicit directives which instruct teachers to behave in a discriminatory way. Policy documents compel nobody, but they do have attached to them rewards and punishments, or benefits and disbenefits. Furthermore, in the United Kingdom documents such as these do not exist.

The second of these is more complicated. This is that these policy documents and the policies which follow from them (not necessarily in a straightforward linear fashion) do not explicitly instruct teachers to behave in a discriminatory way, but they have certain unplanned and unexpected consequences, which means that if teachers follow them, the result is discriminatory, albeit not as intended. In order to try to make sense of our second explanation, we need to say something about the nature of these mechanisms. Could it be that a school needs to classify and normalise (we will leave aside the question of why race should be used in this way) in order to maintain good order and to provide the most conducive conditions (as teachers understand them) for learning. This process works by creating a 'normal' student to which all other students are compared and classified in various ways as departing from such a norm. Indeed, the aim may be to normalise children through various processes of socialisation within the institution. Furthermore, because schooling is a mass procedure and because as a result teachers feel the need to de-differentiate, they do so in terms of a number of fairly simple cultural stereotypes. One of these is racial. Curricula are devised, groupings are arranged, pedagogies are implemented which reflect this principle. There may be other explanations and these can only be tested by careful investigation of the conditions for action at certain set points in time, surfacing the beliefs held by the relevant social actors and understanding how, why and in what way decisions were taken.

Critical Research

We now come to the idea of critical research and we referred earlier to how some commentators (eg. Troyna, 1993) argue that one way of deciding whether research is good or bad is in terms of whether it changes the status quo or makes society a better place. I have already suggested that research cannot be disinterested because the categories which we use to inform ourselves about the world are not universal but socially situated, and the researcher is positioned within various forms of structural constraints and enablements, both institutional and discursive. Furthermore, I have previously argued, following Weber (1974), that research is necessarily involved in politics because when it is made public, it has to, and indeed seeks to, influence the discursive structures of the society. The enlightenment commitment to rationality and Habermas' advocation of undistorted communication in which the latter is judged to be intelligible, truthful, justified and sincere (and it should be noted that for Habermas this prescriptive schema is logically a condition of engaging in any conversation at all) are both committed to a set of values or a way of life. This way of life is normative in that Habermas and others would wish the world to be more like this than it is at present and it is therefore critical of the world as it is.

The argument between Hammersley (1995) and others[63] is therefore between one set of values and another. Hammersley's argument, in short, is that if researchers want to engage in politics, then this is perfectly acceptable, but this should be distinguished from activities which are the sole province of the researcher: they are committed to describing the world, and indeed may have to modify their view of the world in the light of what they find out. The politician on the other hand is not so committed because their activity is centred round an attempt to change the world. Of course, it may be sensible for the politician to understand in a full sense what the world is like before they do this, but it is not essential to have this knowledge in order to move society from what is to what that politician wants it to be. For example, it may be politic to exaggerate about the extent of racial prejudice and discrimination in society (and in a sense it does not matter whether this is correct or incorrect) in order to change that society so that racial prejudice and discrimination cease to exist. Indeed, it may be important to suppress knowledge of what is, if it is judged that it could lead to complacency or resistance, and as a result prevent the politician achieving all they want to achieve.

However, researchers such as Troyna may still want to argue that either both sets of values can be accommodated within a critical researcher model or that research itself (providing descriptions of the world) is inherently and necessarily bound up with values, and that the argument should really be about the credibility of those different sets of values (ie. racism versus non-racism; cultural differentiation versus homogenisation and so forth). All too frequently these two arguments are conflated which inevitably leads to a loss of clarity. There is one further consequence of adopting a position taken up by Gillborn (1998, p. 34, his italics) for example, who suggests that, 'racism operates *through* the work. That is, how qualitative research and critique might, itself, strengthen or defend particular stereotypes and ideologies that further marginalise and pathologise students of ethnic minority background. *Research, whatever its conscious aims and professed values, can be racist.*' He is arguing that because there may be unintended consequences of adopting a particular position (a denial, for instance, that racism is institutionalised in United Kingdom schools), this in itself is racist because it does not in Gillborn's view contribute to the eradication of racial prejudice and discrimination. The logic of this position is that researchers should actively suppress interpretations they want to make if in their opinion the making of them may have detrimental consequences to the anti-racist project to which they are committed. Research is reduced in this sense to polemic. However, Gillborn also wants to act as a researcher in the traditional sense, ie. defend the specific and particular interpretations of the data which he collected. This tension (cf. Hammersley, 1995) is never satisfactorily resolved, and it mirrors a tension in post-modernist explanations between the making of definitive and authoritative statements about forms of knowledge and a refusal to accept universalising modes of thought and global narratives. The next chapter then, examines the influence of post-modern thought on educational discourses.

10 Post-modernism

Power/Knowledge

The theme of this chapter is post-modernism and education, and though the French philosopher, Michael Foucault, is in some ways not representative of thinkers in this field,[64] he does make reference in his work to a wide range of post-modernist themes: the delegitimisation of the transcendental self, the localisation of knowledge, a distaste for universalising modes of thought and global narratives, and a rejection of ethical and teleological ideas. What, in particular, needs to be examined is his central theme of power–knowledge, that is: a particular configuration of the two that would seem to exclude them operating independently. He has argued that:

> Truth is a thing of this world; it is produced only by virtue of multiple forms of constraint. And it induces regular effects of power. Each society has its regimes of truth, its general politics of truth, that is the types of discourse it accepts and makes function as true, the mechanisms and instances which enable one to distinguish true and false statements, the means by which each one is sanctioned, the techniques and procedures accorded value in the acquisition of truth, the status of those who are charged with saying what comes as truth.
>
> (Foucault, 1980, pp. 72–73)

Thus power–knowledge as opposed to power and knowledge or knowledge of power is what is being proposed.

This seems to point to its self-refuting character as an argument. If knowledge of anything only comes about as a result of power arrangements within society, then that knowledge is conditional; or to put it another way, what confidence can we have in the alleged relationship between power and knowledge, when our knowledge of that relationship is subject to power arrangements in society. In addition, the identification of power with knowledge would seem to disallow events, activities, procedures which operate within the rules (the rules of discursive formation) of one episteme being understood within another. This is reinforced in two ways. First, Foucault's notion of genealogy as opposed to archaeology ties closely together discursive formations with power arrangements in society at the time the discursive regime is operating. Second, Foucault is not interested in the human subject as such. The history of ideas has been dominated by the idea of a human subject and a human subject saying something which is taken up in various forms and guises by other people. The traces and connections constitute its history. But Foucault wants to concentrate his critique at the level of concept, idea or text, not person. Thus he would seem to be ruling out the idea that there is such a thing as a human being who can in any way transcend the episteme in which they are positioned, and understanding only occurs in terms of the prevailing arrangements (and this of course includes epistemological arrangements) then in existence.

The third problem is even more serious. Unless we want to distinguish between epistemology and ethics, arguing that the latter has some universal quality, whereas the former is firmly located within particular and specific discursive formations (and he shows no inclination to do so or produce arguments to support a universal theory of value), then he would seem not to be able to distinguish between different regimes of truth or different regimes of power (because that is what they are). He deliberately does not develop a theory of ethics, though it is interesting to note that privately (that is outside of his philosophical work) he was extremely committed (against the death penalty, against inhumane conditions in prison, etc.). So different regimes are only different in kind and not in value. History is cleansed of any teleological or progressive elements. Benign[65] and brutal prison regimes are equally bad or good. Progressive (and I am using this now in a different way) education is no better or worse than educational regimes based on overt forms of fear.

So we are left with three compelling arguments against his notion of power–knowledge: 1) the argument of self-refutation; 2) the argument of paradigmatic incommensurability; 3) the argument of ethical nihilism. Before I address each of these, let me suggest that the argument is compli-cated by other factors. First, there is ample evidence from his whole body of work that he changed his mind, or certainly that he emphasised some aspects at the expense of others at an early stage of his writing and de-emphasised them at a later stage (ie. he republished *Mental Illness and Psychology* with a substantially rewritten second part; his last years were spent on the first stages of the development of an ethical philosophy, some-thing which he set his mind against during most of his working life). Second, the bulk of his writing would seem to suggest that he had little truck with the relativistic element involved in power–knowledge. He was perfectly happy to accept that some truths may be valid across societies, only that methods and occasions of generating truth will ultimately depend on some aspect of a society's power arrangements.

In order to defend him we need to make reference to a well-known distinction in philosophy; between the conditions for the production of truth and the means of its production, or to put it another way, between judgement and procedure. A truth may be produced because of certain arrangements in society (this would refer to issues of access, availability, dissemination, suppression, obfuscation, etc.), but its truth value is not determined or dependent on any of these. This is a tempting way out for Foucault. However, if this were so, it would make redundant the close conjunction of the two terms power and knowledge; indeed, it would make unremarkable the connection he sought to suggest between the two. Second, he may actually be referring to a distinction made by Bhaskar (1989) (see Chapter 2), which is the distinction between epistemology and ontology, in which he argues that epistemology is always transitive and therefore by definition as much a product of prevailing power arrangements in society, but that ontology, certainly with regards to the human sciences, is relatively enduring and thus has a degree of intransitivity about it.[66]

Now, Foucault's defence could take the following form. He is concerned to uncover deeper-lying structures (ie. power, and if we think about this notion, it only seems to be manifest in action or actions, and some manifestations of it are hidden or covert), but knowledge of them, and, of course, of ways of knowing about them are transitive and therefore subject to existing arrangements in society. Now this does not of course provide a solution to the problem of self-refutation. Because this argument is essentially located within the realm of epistemology or knowing (and someone like Popper (1976) would want to argue this),[67] then our knowledge of those mechanisms by which truths are established (and these would include procedural as well as judgemental mechanisms) can necessarily only be limited. These truths are not so much provisional as speculative, partial and incomplete (this is of course Rorty's (1980) defence of epistemic relativism), and that is as far as we can go. The point is that if our knowing is always epistemically relative (and we can never know if it is or not), then how we determine truth from falsehood (and this is of course not procedural but judgemental) must be determined by prevailing power relations in society. If criteria for judgement are universal (that is trans-epistemic), then power relations play a lesser role in judgement, but this is not a synthetic truth but an analytical one. The conclusion simply follows from the premise. As a consequence, it does not tell us anything about the likelihood of those judgemental criteria being universal.

Trans-epistemic Knowledge

This points to the second problem we identified earlier; which is that if we are located within one episteme or one discursive formation, then we literally cannot understand or make sense of ideas, events, activities located epistemologically elsewhere. Foucault developed two methodological approaches. The first is archaeology in which the archaeologist seeks to uncover the epistemological assumptions underlying the formation of ideas in society. In other words, he/she seeks to uncover the rules concerning relations between statements within the discursive formation which allow expression, understanding and use of some ideas to the exclusion of others and, as importantly, the rules concerning the development of the discursive formation. Discursive formations limit the number and type of alternatives. The speaker is positioned by the discursive formation: 'takes up a position that has already been defined'. Foucault (1972) identifies the four stages of the development of a discourse: *the threshold of positivity, the threshold of epistemologisation, the threshold of scientificity* and *the threshold of formalisation*. Archaeology then examines discursive matters. Foucault's later notion of genealogy examines relations between discursive and non-discursive matters, or between ideas and power relations in society.

A number of points about this need to be made. First, he argues that archaeology cannot operate outside of discursive relations which are situated in time and place. It does not and cannot operate 'independently of all discourse or all objects of discourse'. However, this seems to be merely a covering note. We are told that these are the stages through which a discourse goes during an evolutionary path. Not just that all discourses in the past have fitted this pattern, but that this pattern will be sustained in the future. Foucault in his *Archaeology of Knowledge* (one of his earlier works) had yet to develop fully his notion of genealogy in which these discursive formations and their evolution would be more firmly located within power arrangements in society or within non-discursive formations. Though these matters concern discourse and ideas within discursive formations, they are not ideological or necessarily located in systems of ideas, but have a material base. They are in effect nomothetic; this is how society works. They are examples of Bhaskar's mechanisms but expressed as epistemological forms. The difficulty comes as to whether they are relatively, absolutely or briefly enduring and if not what is their status: merely historical artefacts? And, second, since we have knowledge of them and furthermore knowledge of a method by which they can be discovered, is this epistemological knowledge briefly, relatively or absolutely enduring?

The next problem associated with this is more serious. Does Foucault have a method?[68] And what underpins his method? He certainly has a theory of time, or more precisely a theory of causation. Some events can be placed before other events and are responsible for bringing them into being. He has a theory of association – some events can be shown to correlate with others. He has a theory of significance – some events have a greater relevance to the development of theory than others; and finally he has a theory of reference – ideas refer to real objects, ie. power relations. If method was absolutely located within an episteme, then it could not be used to identify events, activities of a different epistemic nature. If human beings are located within discursive formations which exclude them from certain ideas and these discursive formations are located historically, then are all those historically located human beings operating under the same epistemic spell at the same time? When one episteme gives way to another, does this mean we see things differently in every way? By introducing an historical method to describe the formation of discourse, Foucault has settled for a transcendental mechanism which seems to have the status of an a-historical truth.

I referred earlier to the problem of finding a consistent reading of the whole of Foucault's writings, and here, it seems to me, is an example of that inconsistency. On the one hand he suggests that knowledge of everything is related to power arrangements in society, and on the other, he describes certain mechanisms for the production of discourse which seem not to relate to any particular and specific arrangements of power. In order to cite the Bhaskar defence I outlined earlier, he would have to argue that knowledge of these rules is transitive, a position he seems reluctant to take. And the reason he has to take this position is because he wants to discuss arrangements in different epistemes and make comparisons between them. He can only do this from one perspective, his own epistemic perspective; but presumably the historical or archaeological method which is located within his own epistemic perspective is going to produce different types of truth about different epistemic arrangements and therefore the comparison certainly becomes invalid. His insistence on tying closely together discursive formations with specific historical periods means that the subsequent account of human societies is, as Archer (1988) argues, too all-encompassing. She refers to this as 'the myth of cultural integration', and she argues that it has created 'an archetype of culture(s) as the perfectly woven system, in which every element was interdependent with every other – the ultimate exemplar of compact and coherent organisation' (Archer, 1988, p. 2).

Ethical Nihilism

The main problem is the reduction involved in his account of human beings. As we have noted already, the history of ideas is stripped of people. In their place are concepts, ideas, texts, mechanisms. Again this has contributed to the third of our critiques – that of ethical nihilism (Taylor, 1998).[69] By refusing to take up specific political and ethical positions, he is forced to treat all power formations as equal. Power becomes a monolithic concept:

> . . . Because it is produced from one moment to the next, at every point, or rather in relation from one point to another. Power is everywhere . . . because it comes from everywhere.
>
> (Foucault, 1979, p. 93)

This goes beyond the ethical. It is not just that, within the framework offered by Foucault, one cannot judge between different regimes of power, it is that this notion of power becomes singularly unhelpful in explicating different degrees and types of power exercised on and by human beings. A word that covers everything refers to nothing and has no explanatory usefulness. So if we compare progressive and non-progressive ideologies,[70] since both are equally power-imbued, we cannot distinguish between them. That is we cannot distinguish between them at the explanatory level. Clearly they refer to different phenomena, but Foucault's notion of power cannot allow us to make interesting and valid comparisons between the two. If power is present in all human interaction, it becomes impossible to distinguish between the different instances of its application. The essential ingredient that is missing is that some people possess more power than others, or to put it in another way, power is differentially distributed. Furthermore, unless we have some notion of agency, we are in danger of reducing human beings to the role of 'unwitting dupes' of structural forces beyond their comprehension and influence.

There is of course a way out for Foucault from this dilemma and he appears to take it when he suggests that:

> One has to dispense with the constituent subject, to get rid of the subject itself . . . [in order] to arrive at an analysis which can account for the constitution of the subject within an historical framework . . . a form of history which can account for the constitution of knowledges, discourses, domains of objects, etc. without having to make reference to a subject which . . . runs its empty sameness throughout the course of history.
>
> (Foucault, 1980, p. 117)

Clearly the social actor (this term is being used here in a very non-Foucauldian sense) may be located within various constructing mechanisms, whether of a 'governmentality' kind or otherwise; and these subjectivities have to be understood as being in history and therefore subject to change. However, this does not solve our earlier problem which may be expressed as follows: if the self is constructed in different ways historically and this comprises the way the person understands the world, and if that construction denies them the possibility of thinking differently, social actors can only understand past selves (not their own, but other peoples') through the lens of their own. Unless Foucault is prepared to forego this disclaimer, when he argues that he does not want to understand the subject as 'transcendental in relation to the fields of events' (Foucault, 1980, p. 117), then he cannot account for trans-epistemic knowledge. In short, he would seem to have undermined his whole project. On the other hand, the self may be understood as only partially constituted by those networks of power, which, whether initiated by governments or other people, have the effect of allowing the individual to think and see in one particular way and not in another. In other words, any social theory (again Foucault perhaps would have abjured such a term) has to allow for the possibility of its transformation and the transformation of its objects (including epistemic ones). This is not intended to minimise the powerful influence Foucault has had in the social sciences and amongst educational researchers, but it is to point to the inconsistencies and contradictions which occasionally confront us in reading him.

A Theory of Ethics

However, in reality, Foucault did have a view of ethics, which was not purely descriptive but was intended to proscribe various forms of behaviour, even if it is only the behaviour of the individual concerned. He remarks that:

> There is always something ludicrous in philosophical discourse when it tries, from the outside, to dictate for others, to tell them where their truth is and how to find it, or when it works up a case against them in the language of naive positivity. But it is entitled to explore what might be changed, in its own thought, through a practice of knowledge that is foreign to it.
>
> (Foucault, 1983, p. 9)

We may call it an ethic, not just because it proscribes behaviour, ie. by indicating how he, himself, intends to behave, but also because he recommends that behaviour for everyone.[71] He is identifying a number of virtues here, for example, honesty, reflexive examination and openness in a universal sense. However much he pleads for a 'self-conscious theoretical modesty' (Blacker, 1998, p. 361), it would seem impossible to ignore the fact that he is making reference to a preferred way of living, or, to put it another way, an ethic of being. He goes further than this, and suggests that his ethical project comprises four modes. The first of these is *the determination of the ethical substance* for the individual subject. This would constitute the focus of concern – the aspect of life which needs to be worked on. The second of these is a proper understanding of the way one is *positioned in relation to those rules which constitute the subject matter.* Blacker (1998, p. 362), for instance, suggests that 'this entails an examination into one's very concern for truth, a consciousness of how one partakes in truth's manufacture'. This is the act of genealogy performed on oneself. The third mode is *ethical work* or training the self to behave in a certain way. This is the most difficult of the operations and entails the application of virtues such as honesty, endurance, perseverance and so forth. Finally, there is *the teleological stage*. For Foucault, this constitutes a new self-mastery. This involves resisting the forms of subjectification which previously the self was a part of. It has two implications. The first is an acknowledgement of the possibility of transcendental behaviour. It is being suggested here that the self can operate outside of those networks of power which constitute society and that a version of the self, though never trans-epistemic in any meaningful sense, still has credence. The second implication is that the ethical project which has just been described comprises both an end or teleology and a procedure. This would suggest the possibility of progress in human affairs, something which Foucault fiercely resisted in much of his work. This notion of progress and how it impacts on educational ends needs to be examined further.

Foucault did suggest at various times that the enlightenment project, which understands history as movement from a state of ignorance to a state of knowledge through the adoption of scientific procedures, is misguided. For example, what we take to be more humane forms of punishment replacing more brutalising ones is in fact two sides of the same coin. The former may be more efficient in the sense that self-policing always works better in the construction of the self and of populations, but it is not better in any ethical sense. In other words, it does not constitute or show progress in human affairs. Likewise, the examination which was conceived as a more enlightened form of social ordering because it was fair to everyone in fact constitutes another type of oppressive behaviour, all the more oppressive because it seems to embrace a set of ethical procedures. Again, Foucault repeatedly warned against understanding it as a form of progress.

In order to make sense of this debate, we need to distinguish between necessary and contingent flaws in the humanistic project of cumulative progress that societies inevitably make. If, as Foucault suggests, the humanistic discourse, understood as a more enlightened set of practices, in fact comprises an equally unenlightened set of practices with what went before, then, as a result, this *doxa*, or indeed any other, cannot sustain or make sense of the idea of an ethical theory. However, he may be saying something which is very different. For instance, Blacker (1998, p. 351) suggests that it is indeed the latter position to which Foucault subscribes: 'For Foucault the ideals associated with humanism are not inherently contradictory, but genealogy reveals that their consequential deeds always seem to belie their words.' It is a matter of history that little progress has in fact been made, not that progress per se is impossible.[72] It is a contingent fact about the world that self-interest, greed and ignorance thwart the best-laid humanistic plans. However, if it is the latter interpretation of his theory which is correct, then Foucault is not ruling out the possibility of progress, even if it is of a type which many in modern societies would not agree is appropriate.

Foucault's view of that enlightened state would therefore seem to be one of resisting those forms of control which act to enslave, and the project is a self-consciously reflexive one.

Controlling Populations and Examinations

What therefore can we recover from the numerous writings of Foucault for the study of education (and it has to be said that many of the criticisms made in this chapter also apply to other theorists in the post-modernist tradition)? What we can recover is an extraordinarily vibrant sociology of educational and epistemological forms. For example, his work on examinations in *Discipline and Punish: The Birth of the Prison* (Foucault, 1979) has the effect of allowing them to be understood in a different way. Previously, the examination was thought of as a progressive mechanism for combatting nepotism, favouritism and arbitrariness, and for contributing to the more efficient workings of society. The examination was considered to be a reliable and valid way for choosing the appropriate members of a population for the most important roles in society. As part of the procedure a whole apparatus or technology was constructed which was intended to legitimise it. This psychometric framework, though continually in a state of flux, has served as a means of support for significant educational programmes in the twentieth century, ie. the establishment of the tripartite system in the United Kingdom after the Second World War, and continues to underpin educational reforms since 1979. Though purporting to be a scientific discourse, the theory itself is buttressed by a number of un-examined principles. These comprise: a particular view of competence; a notion of hierarchy; a way of understanding human nature and a cor-respondence idea of truth. Furthermore, the idea of the examination is firmly located within a discourse of progression: society is progressively and teleologically becoming one with reason as its descriptive apparatus is refined and as it moves closer to a complete version of reality.

On the other hand, for Foucault (1979, p. 184) the examination 'com-bines the techniques of an observing hierarchy and those of a normalising judgement. It is a normalising gaze, a surveillance that makes it possible to qualify, to classify and to punish. It establishes over individuals a visibility through which one differentiates them and judges them.' The examination therefore does not just describe what is, but allows society to construct indi-viduals in certain ways and in the process organises itself. Knowledge of persons is thus created in particular ways which has the effect of binding individuals to each other, embedding those individuals in networks of power and sustaining mechanisms of surveillance which are all the more powerful because they work by allowing individuals to police themselves:

One often speaks of the ideology that the human 'sciences' bring with them, in either discrete or prolix manner. But does their very technology, this tiny operational schema that has become so widespread (from psychiatry to pedagogy, from the diagnosis of diseases to the hiring of labour), this familiar method of the examination, implement. Within a single mechanism, power relations that make it possible to extract and constitute knowledge? It is not simply at the level of consciousness, of representations and in what one thinks one knows, but at the level of what makes possible the knowledge that is transformed into political investment.

(Foucault, 1979, p. 185)

The examination, according to Foucault, introduced a whole new mechanism which both contributed to a new type of knowledge formation and constructed a new network of power, all the more persuasive once it had become established throughout society. This mechanism worked in three ways: 1) by transforming 'the economy of visibility into the exercise of power' (ibid., p. 187); 2) by introducing 'individuality into the field of documentation' (ibid., p. 189); and 3) by making 'each individual a "case"' (ibid., p. 191). In the first instance, disciplinary power is exercised invisibly and this contrasts with the way power networks in the past operated visibly, through perhaps the naked exercise of force. This invisibility works by imposing on subjects a notion of objectivity which acts to bind examined persons to a truth about that examination, a truth which is hard to resist. The examined person understands him or herself in terms of criteria which underpin that process, not least that they are successful or unsuccessful. The examination therefore works by 'arranging objects' (ibid., p. 187) or people in society. In the second instance, the examination allows the individual to be archived by being inscribed in a variety of documents which fixes and captures them. Furthermore, it is possible to understand this process even when the rhetoric of what is being implemented is progressive and benign. Over the last fifteen years in United Kingdom schools, the proliferation and extension of assessment through such devices as key stage tests, records of achievement, examined coursework, education certificates and school reports *and* evaluation through such devices as school inspection, teacher appraisal, profiles and the like means that teachers and students are increasingly subject to disciplinary regimes of individual measurement and assessment which has the further effect of fixing them as cases. The third of Foucault's modalities then is when the individual becomes an object for a branch of knowledge: 'The case is no longer, as in casuistry or jurisprudence, a set of circumstances, defining an act and capable of modifying the application of a rule; it is the individual as he (sic) may be described, judged, measured, compared with others, in his very individuality; and it is also the individual who has to be trained or corrected, classified, normalized, excluded, etc.' (ibid., p. 191). One final point needs to be made about the examination, as Foucault understands it, and this is that for the first time the individual can be scientifically and objectively categorised and characterised through a modality of power where difference becomes the most relevant factor. Hierarchical normalisation becomes the dominant way of organising society.

Though as Rorty (1986) argues, Foucault's contribution to epistemology is limited,[73] this should not detract from the importance of his sociology of forms, particularly in respect of educational systems, discourses and modalities. In this chapter, I have suggested that Foucault's attempts to confront the problems of self-refutation, the legitimacy of trans-epistemic knowledge and the possibility of constructing an ethical framework were only partially successful. However, he was during his lifetime able to sketch out an agenda which has implications for how we should approach the understanding of educational activities and systems. The last chapter in this book therefore attempts to explain what this educational discourse which has been central to this and other chapters might be.

11 Afterthoughts: Changing Knowledge of Relatively Unchanging Entities

Throughout this book I have emphasised the irreducibility of social structures and relations to explanations or theoretical constructs. If some notion of human agency is to be preserved, it is also necessary to avoid reifying social properties. However, there is a more serious problem for educational researchers, which is that regardless of whether a theory about human relations is true or not at a particular point in time, it may become true later, because it then becomes the accepted way of proceeding in society. Its truth value is thus not a function of its original correctness as a theory to explain some aspect of human life, but a function of how particular communities of people construct and reconstruct forms of knowledge. Furthermore, it would be wrong to construe those people as living falsely or in a misguided way because the subject matter of social and educational enquiry is in part those beliefs and frameworks which constitute social life. Thus it is possible to suggest that the 'real', of which this book has been much concerned, is only real at particular moments of time. Giddens (1984) coins the phrase 'virtual reality', but this, I feel, fails to capture the essence of the matter because it seems to indicate a reversion to idealism. For Bhaskar (1989) these structures, mechanisms or entities anyway only have a relatively enduring life-span and thus his notion of 'unchanging entities' seems to need, as he acknowledges himself, some modification.[74]

What of course complicates the picture is the epistemological dimension, or the capacity of social researchers to know the world. What has been consistently argued throughout this book has been the inability of researchers and indeed observers to step outside those frameworks of understanding through which the self is constructed. In other words, values and more importantly an understanding of those values are essential dimensions to the research enterprise. This is further complicated by how the self is constructed. Enlightenment thinking seemed to suggest that the self could be construed as the one sure and certain locus of understanding. It was not possible to doubt this essential core. However, if essentialist, religious, deterministic or reductionist versions are set aside, it is possible to understand the self as a reflexive project (Giddens, 1991). There is no intention here to suggest that the self is engaged in a search for some ultimate purpose. However, it is to suggest that the self is always engaged in a process of reflexive monitoring of its actions and this is inevitably a response to particular understandings of the world. What is real, even if mediated through the value systems of human beings, is thus an essential referent for the reflexive project. Furthermore, this reflexivity acts, in conjunction with other modes and forms of reflexivity, to construct the world. It is in this sense that reality is constructed, though this is far from suggesting that object and subject are separate or that the subject could adopt a god's-eye view of reality by bracketing out those forms which constitute them as persons and in society.

The Construction of Knowledge

If this is correct, then we also need to make reference to those forms of life which have epistemic significance. Modern societies have constructed elaborate and complicated systems for determining truth from falsehood. One of these is the university. In an earlier chapter I referred to the way disciplinary knowledge is endlessly subject to reconfigurations of the spaces between different groups of knowledge makers, and that these temporary structures have weak and strong boundaries between them. I also made reference to the role of argument, conversation and invective (a characteristic power strategy) in settling disputes, both of a methodological and substantive kind. The example referred to was that of race; ie. Gillborn's (1998) characterisation of his opponents as 'racist', even though he concedes that their intention was not to act in this way. (His argument is that their project is racist because it de-racialises understanding of educational activities and institutions.) Another manifestation of these mechanisms is the commodification of research which is partly a consequence of the imposition of reductionist frameworks which attempt to quantify researcher output through such means as the Research Assessment Exercise in United Kingdom universities.

A fourth example concerns the way universities are developing professional doctorates. More than thirty universities in the United Kingdom are now offering professional education doctorates. These are intended to provide an alternative to PhD study and comprise taught courses (assessed by assignment) and a thesis. The taught courses typically include research method courses, courses on professionalism and subject-specific courses in fields such as management, curriculum, assessment, policy and school improvement. They may be targeted (for example, the Bristol EdD), general (London Institute of Education EdD) or taught through distance learning (Open University EdD). All are designed to offer professional training which relates to the concerns of educational practitioners (ie. senior managers in schools and colleges, Local Education Authority officers, policy-makers at local and national levels). What characterises them is a tension between academic and professional knowledge and the clear desire to professionalise the doctorate; that is, appropriate professional knowledge as worthy of study. The university itself is increasingly being influenced by policy-driven interventions of the state, new forms of communication, its marginalisation from the centre of the knowledge industry, 'non-jurisdictionally bounded global discourses' (Yeatman, 1990) and by 'crises in disciplinarity and professionalism' (Brennan, 1998).[75]

Indeed, Stronach and MacLure (1997) identify in this context three types of games. The first (Game 1) is traditional with research involving a lengthy apprenticeship. Research takes place over a long time period and is framed within recognisable and accepted research frameworks. It embodies many of the characteristics of modernity such as teleology and essentialism. It makes assumptions about the nature of knowledge and posits correct procedures for understanding the world. This has been progressively replaced by Game 2 systems which are driven by state interventions in research environments. Game 2 strategies comprise an acceleration in the traditional practices of doing research and they involve compromise and rationalisation, driven by a shortage of time and money. Citation becomes an important strategy, though the issues to which the citation refers are not incorporated into the actual practice of research. Game 3 on the other hand is driven by the dominant business ethos and bears little resemblance to Game 1. Researchers are detached from the knowledge community which supports them and which has in the past provided legitimation for their activities. Research tenders specify approaches and strategies which are to be adopted if the researcher is to be awarded the contract. The researcher is reduced to a technician, is usually employed on a short-term contract by the university (an example perhaps of the university professing to adopt a Game 1 framework while at the same time undermining it) and is insecure and demoralised (cf. Lee, 1998). This managerial or business-orientated discourse is therefore rapidly becoming the norm with subsequent implications for the idea of the university itself. All these are examples of those mechanisms which act to construct knowledge, though it is important to understand the university as only one player in the game. Other agencies in society act to produce and reproduce epistemic valuations. However, what is important to emphasise is the way power is ever present in these constructions.

It is present in four different ways. First, research takes place in settings and environments in which social actors are differently distributed and have different access to resources. The subject matter of research is those differences and this means that power is a necessary construct in explanations of social life. Second, the researcher is a part of those networks of power and at times will be in more powerful and less powerful relations with the social actors in the environments which they are studying. Social research is therefore always valued research 'in that both the values of participants in the research and the values of the researcher themselves are central to the construction of research texts' (Scott and Usher, 1999, p. 1). However, there are more profound reasons as to why power is central to any research activity and this is that research inevitably represents a closure (sometimes quite arbitrary) of the way the world is being represented. This representation or research text acts to fix reality in a particular way which is never entirely justified and cannot be legitimated by reference to a notion of what the world is really like. The act of closure itself is a part of the reality which the researcher is trying to describe. The fourth reason is more important still. By adopting a particular way of working, a particular understanding of epistemology and ontology, the researcher is of course rejecting or turning aside from other frameworks and this itself is an act of power: 'since in education there is no single correct research procedure and no superordinate methodology, power relations feature in and between research traditions' (ibid.). An example of these networks of power central to the creation of knowledge is the field of curriculum[76] and how it was and perhaps should be constructed.

Curriculum Studies

We start with an attempt to specify the different ways by which curriculum studies may be understood. There are a number of possibilities and each makes reference to a particular cohering element.

1 *Subject matter* – A curriculum specialist would be committed to the study of the curriculum, as it is constructed, enacted and evaluated in various educational environments. The argument of integration would then take the following form: the study of the curriculum would consist of a focus on a set of issues which are relevant to a study of education (policy deliberation, policy delivery, pedagogy and evaluation, for example), and about the types/strengths of the boundaries between this and other forms of knowledge.

2 *Epistemology* – Curriculum specialists would share a common epistemology; that is, a similar way of understanding educational issues. This might take the form of an agreement about how to resolve the theory–practice problematic; the place of values in curriculum-making and implementation; the extent of the constructed nature of the curriculum; and the correct way of reaching agreement about appropriate values in society.

3 *Methodology* – Curriculum specialists would share a common methodological position to examine the social and educational world. This might take the form of a positivist/empiricist framework in which the principles

of phenomenalism, nominalism, value neutrality and universal method are understood as central to the research act; or a hermeneutic/interpretivist epistemology in which the values of the researcher and the values of the researched are prioritised; or a critical realist stance in which epistemology and ontology are carefully separated, and an acknowledgement made that the former is essentially transitive whereas the latter comprises relatively enduring structures; or a post-modern/idealist perspective which denies we can study reality as such.

4 *Oppositional construct* – One further position that curriculum specialists could take is to define themselves in opposition to some other ways of understanding educational activities. This could take the form of opposition to another form of knowledge (and the opposition to this could take an epistemological, methodological or even content orientation); or opposition to a common-sense version of education (that educational processes do not work in the way they are perceived to work by most people in society); or opposition to a political perspective (because they may have methodological, epistemological or normative disagreements with policy-makers).

I have argued previously that the boundaries, and the degree of insulation, between different forms of knowledge determine what can or cannot be said about education and therefore about how educational processes are understood in society. Further, I have argued that description of educational activities at present is dominated by (not least in policy-making fora) a technicist view of education, a tacit acceptance of the need to centralise decision-making, a sectionalist view of educational deliberation, a behavioural-objectives view of curriculum, a behaviourist view of human behaviour, a reductionist methodology which determines how it is viewed and how the discourse is constructed, a marginalisation of debates about the aims and objectives of education, and a misunderstanding of the equity debate. Whichever of the four possible stances is adopted, it is enough to suggest here that each is implicated in particular struggles over what constitutes acceptable knowledge.

In this chapter, curriculum is used in a wide sense to indicate both the formal curriculum and the curriculum in action. In the first case, therefore, study of the curriculum comprises both the way it is constructed by curriculum-makers and the way it is understood by curriculum-implementors. In the second case, it comprises the way the curriculum is implemented – the curriculum in use – and it therefore relates fundamentally to pedagogy and outcomes. A number of assumptions will be made. The first of these is that a curriculum is always a selection from an almost infinite number of items (content), from a range of possible aims and objectives (purpose) and is underpinned by a view of how the recipient should be constructed within it, of how teachers should behave towards those recipients and fundamentally of how knowledge should be conceived. The second is that a curriculum is more or less coherent; this being understood as whether it incorporates a range of ideological positions which may or may not conflict. This refers to the curriculum as text and it is hardly unsurprising that many curricula comprise conflicting message systems when they are frequently constructed and reconstructed by groups of people with different interests. The curriculum itself has both a form and a content. In the former case, it seeks to position its reader so that it is read in one way and one way only; in the latter case, it acts by excluding a body or domain of knowledge which may or may not be appropriate to the model held by the practitioner. The third assumption that is made is that any curriculum text refers implicitly or explicitly to other curriculum texts, both presently used and in the past, and to other relations in society. The curriculum is therefore a selection from what is available, intertextually situated, has a history and is socially constructed.

Classification

A curriculum framework furthermore is strongly or weakly classified (Bernstein, 1971), where in the first case the boundaries between knowledge domains are tightly maintained and in the second case, loosely maintained. Whether it is strongly or loosely classified is determined by the progenitors of that curriculum framework and more importantly by micro-political processes which affect the relay within the policy cycle. A strongly classified curriculum may comprise a number of possible domains and arrangements, but what it reflects is not what these domains are, but the strength of the boundary classifications between them. This type of curriculum framework may be contrasted with one in which the boundaries between knowledge domains are looser, and this is reflected in both the public face of that curriculum framework and in its underlying purposes and aspirations. Teachers, furthermore, are positioned differently in the two types of curricula – in the first case their professional lives are conducted within a narrow range of opinions and their immediate source of intellectual support is from other specialists within their area; in the second case, their professional lives are conducted within more loosely framed coalitions of fellow practitioners, which are more likely to be in a continuous state of formation and reformation.

We have identified two ends of a spectrum, what Fogarty (1991a, b) calls a fragmented disciplinary approach (strong classification) and a more networked approach to curriculum planning (weak classification). Within this spectrum, however, Fogarty identifies a range of other positions:[77]

- *Connected* – An attempt is made to relate isolated parts of a domain to parts of other domains. These connections may be retrospective or prospective.
- *Nested* – Here generic skills are isolated from the content of each domain and understood as cross-curricular. Thus a certain type of inductive analysis may be thought of as appropriate in both mathematics and sociology lessons.
- *Sequenced* – Topics within each domain may be deliberately sequenced so that children are then able to use their knowledge of them within separate domains. Spatial mapping may be taught to children at an early age so that later they can use this skill in more advanced mathematics and geography classrooms.
- *Shared* – The content of any one domain at a particular stage in the child's learning programme refers to the content of another domain at the same time. The general focus, for example, may be the Vikings. However, within this general theme, each domain of the curriculum focuses on aspects of it which its practitioners would consider to be central to their concerns. The history teacher may focus on key events in the Viking invasion of Britain, the cookery teacher may concentrate on the type of diet enjoyed by the Vikings, the language teacher may focus on the preponderance of Viking words in the English language, and so forth.
- *Webbed* – This is a more complicated version of the shared curriculum. Instead of an event or activity acting as the cohering link, a theme is proposed which may be treated in different ways in the different domains. That it will be treated differently is a function of the rules and criteria which have been developed over time by that disciplinary domain. So, for example, psychology, sociology and biology teachers may all choose to address the theme of the nature of knowledge but present to their students different epistemological models. As Kysilka (1998, p. 200) argues: 'The disciplines remain intact, the content of the disciplines is not changed, but the teachers make a special effort to address the theme' in different ways 'as they individually work with the students on the content to be learnt.'
- *Threaded* – The link which is made here between the subject domains is in terms of the process of learning and not thematic or content similarities. The curriculum framework is constructed through a series of specific intellectual skills, and their pedagogy is realised through specific content embedded in subject domains. Each subject domain is therefore understood as a vehicle for the delivery of a set of skills which may be illustrated within each domain through a variety of content. Content in each domain is therefore chosen, not because it reflects the principles and criteria underpinning that domain, but

because it most appropriately reflects the cross-curricular skills identified as of prior importance to content domain knowledge.

- *Integrated* – Here the boundaries between the domains are considerably weakened as teachers abandon their disciplinary orientation and seek to provide a curriculum which integrates knowledge. An example of this could be *Man, A Course of Study* (MACOS) developed by Jerome Bruner and others in the 1970s which sought to examine the sociality of human beings through a coherent and ideologically explicit discussion of their activities in the world. Two points need to be made here. First, it achieved its coherence by adopting an explicit epistemological and onto-logical perspective which was at the time heavily criticised by other academics and practitioners embedded within their own disciplinary perspectives. Second, though MACOS breached the boundaries between the various social science domains, it left relatively intact the boundary between natural and social science domains.
- *Immersed* – Here the student is deliberately positioned by the curriculum text in a loose and fragmented way. The strength of the boundaries between domains is established to allow its framing (Bernstein, 1971) to be deliberately loosened. We will see later how a loosely classified curriculum may still be taught in a strongly framed way. Immersion, however, allows students to construct their own integrated curriculum from different content areas.

Framing

We now come to the second of Bernstein's message systems – how the curriculum is framed by the actions of teachers and pupils. We begin by making a distinction between knowledge per se and pedagogic knowledge. If classification involves the selection and subsequent ordering of knowledge into domains and if this is a social activity, framing in a similar manner comprises a selection and subsequent ordering of knowledge for pedagogic reasons. A number of principles are at work and these guide the choices that are made. The most important of these is progression.

Underpinning the notion of progression is that there is a rationale for teaching some aspects of the knowledge domain before others and that a subject can in fact be arranged in a reliable hierarchy. Adey (1997) argues that it is possible to do this and develops a three-dimensional model comprising conceptual complexity, breadth and extent. For Adey (1997, p. 370), 'the breadth dimension indicates the range of different topics – which may be more or less grouped into subjects – about which the person has some knowledge'; whereas the extent dimension 'shows how much knowledge the person has about each topic'. Using these last two dimensions only to understand curriculum dimension leads to a naive view of learning. For Adey, a measure of conceptual complexity is also needed to provide a fully developed model of curriculum progression. A number of possibilities have been suggested and these range from Piagetian (1971) complexity in terms of movement from concrete operational to formal operational thinking, to Kohlberg's (1976) stages of moral thought where the subject progresses from pre-moral and conventional rule conformity levels to the acceptance of general rights and standards and even to adopting individual principles of conduct. Dickinson and Lee (1978) likewise develop a progressive hierarchy in the field of history education, where their notion of conceptual complexity involves movement from a less detached and restricted view of a situation to greater detachment and the adoption of a more comprehensive viewpoint. These hierarchies are based on empirical investigation: the claim is therefore made that this is how children naturally progress. The other way of establishing knowledge hierarchies is through some form of logical ordering. Here, it is suggested that complexity comprises both a progressive development of more items of knowledge and the making of more complicated connections between these items of knowledge. Undoubtedly, the various hierarchies referred to above have been constructed with reference to both claims.

It is pertinent at this stage to examine in more detail these claims, leaving to one side for the time being the conflation of logical and empirical elements in the argument. Piaget's three-stage model begins with a discussion of concrete operations which comprise the ability to quantify and identify similarities in objects which are different and an early awareness of the ability to predict based on observed patterns. Stage two comprises a progressive development of these skills where the child is better able to classify and construct taxonomies and make comparisons between objects. Stage three, the stage of formal or abstract thinking, includes the ability to exclude, separate or combine variables in approaching problems and the ability to formulate hypotheses which can then be tested empirically. This stage also includes meta-analysis in that the child is able to focus on those operations which underpin and drive thinking as such – it is not the substantive matter which is of concern but the way the child deals with it.[78]

Kohlberg's stages of moral thought begin with a discussion of the pre-moral level where the child is only orientated to punishment and obedience but fairly rapidly moves on to an appreciation of reward. This naive instrumental hedonism is pre-moral in that moral considerations do not enter into the child's thinking. Stages three and four comprise levels of conventional rule conformity. Good behaviour is at first defined as that which is approved by others, and it then becomes progressively more formal by a fixed orientation to authority, rules and the maintenance of the social order. Concepts such as duty and respect for authority are considered to be important here. Finally, the child/adult progresses to a higher level of moral consciousness where moral principles become progressively internalised and understood as constructed by society. This is a legalistic framework. The highest state of moral consciousness is where principles are abstracted and ethicised and dependent on individual conscience.

Historical models of development (Dickinson and Lee, 1978) likewise move from the child at level one understanding facts as separate and not related to each other. The child struggles to establish relationships between these facts. At level two, the child's mental operations are dominated by egocentricity where he or she fails to isolate their own personal prejudice or involvement in the subject matter and adopts a less than objective or detached viewpoint. Level three is then a more detached perspective, but even here the child fails to understand that there are a number of possible perspectives on the world. At level four, the child is able both to adopt a more detached viewpoint and make connections to embrace a more all-encompassing view of history.

The question we need to ask is whether it is possible to designate these progressive hierarchies as natural and therefore cross-cultural or whether in fact (especially if they have been developed by observation of how children presently learn in particular cultures) they are ways of ordering conceptual complexity developed by particular educational regimes at particular time points and in particular places.[79] If they are in fact the latter, then we have to be aware of the place of values in the designation of curriculum content and curriculum progression between items of content. Empirical research may inform us about how children learn within certain time- and place-specific arrangements for education and more importantly about some of the consequences (both planned and unplanned) of adopting particular curricula. What it cannot do, however, is suggest that these constitute a natural state of being, which would need to be taken account of regardless of the circumstances in which the child is being educated. The normative dimension can only be articulated by reference to the aims and purposes of education within particular communities of knowledge-makers.

The Discourse of Education

However, it is not enough simply to describe research as a powerful activity, it is also a moral activity, in the sense that researchers are normatively implicated in the research texts they produce, and how they do this involves them in making ethical decisions. Macintyre (1988) uses the term 'moral agency' and contrasts this with being in thrall to social structures. In particular, he suggests that one common response to structural imperatives by academic researchers is to compartmentalise their different lives; so, for example, an academic may position themselves in relation to their chosen area of study in a particular way and then occupy a different position when it comes to applying that knowledge to their own professional practice. Macintyre sees certain dangers in this approach since this has the tendency to fragment the reflexive project which people are engaged in. He suggests that the knowledge gatherer or the moral agent should be seeking to live virtuously and in doing so pay careful attention to two dispositions, those of consistency and integrity. This is of course difficult to achieve, but it is especially significant for those engaged in educational research because education itself is a moral activity. It is therefore important to close this book by identifying some characteristics of this educational discourse.

It has a symbiotic relationship with practice. It is not a pure discipline like mathematics, in that the problems which are being solved now could have been solved two thousand years ago (this argument comes with the proviso that certain technological developments such as computers allow the solving of problems which could not have been solved then). The point, however, is that there is nothing in the world itself which compels mathematics to work in certain ways. An applied discipline such as education is always concerned with theorising practice as it is, and moreover the means of that theorising, the conceptual and methodological tools to do it, are part of the way particular societies and therefore particular education systems are constructed. There is a further complication, which is that there is a symbiotic relationship between theory and practice. Practice dictates how and what can be said about education and theory influences practice, whether that theory is correct or not.

The second characteristic of educational theorising is that unlike many other pure and applied disciplines, the study of education is itself educational. If we study the life cycle of geese, we may become better informed about how geese behave; what we do not become is more geese-like. We do not seek to take on the characteristics of those animate beings we are studying. However, if we are studying the way human beings learn, we are necessarily concerned in a reflexive manner with our own learning. That is, I am not arguing the merely tautological, but I am suggesting that this reflexive orientation takes on a particular hue when our activity mirrors the subject of our study.

The third characteristic is that education has a necessary relationship with practical politics and policy-making. The evaluative function of educational theorising is about the making of judgements. These judgements may be related to norms about how educational systems should be constructed, whether by policy-makers or researchers. What is at stake here is the intermingling of the descriptive and the normative – a judgement about what is lacking in some prescriptive sense. I have argued throughout that description per se is never possible in the social sciences – that any text produced about the social world is necessarily imbued with value. Various attempts have been made to argue against this position; one of which was described in a previous chapter. (A notion of effectiveness has been constructed which it is claimed, does not involve the researcher in either making value judgements or incorporating their own values into the act of describing educational activities. In fact, if we look more closely, it is possible to see that the definition of the construct and the methodology appropriated are infused with a particular educational philosophy and a set of educational values.) If then, we are making value judgements all the time, we are involved in the power relations which characterise policy-making. There is a further argument that, since our knowledge is both prescriptive and relevant to policy-making about education, we cannot escape responsibility for the political implications of what we do. Suffice it here to suggest that educational researchers should both seek to influence policy-makers and that the business of policy-making is a legitimate subject for educational researchers to study.

The fourth characteristic of educational theorising is the particular difficulty it has with establishing nomothetic explanations of practice. This is a necessary consequence of educational theorising. Any criteria for determining what is or is not good research are disputed. There are a number of ways by which educational researchers seek to validate their conclusions: 1) by seeking to develop a correct method – this allows the research community to argue that, if it is correctly applied, a truthful account of educational activities emerges; 2) by making judgements about the relevance and usefulness of the findings; 3) by establishing a system of peer review which allows the research community to come to an agreement about what is good research and what is not. All these systems have been credited with problems. In the first case, researchers disagree about what is an appropriate method in the social sciences, with some arguing that value-impregnated stances are legitimate and others arguing that the values of the researcher should be bracketed out from the enterprise. Equally, some have argued that truthful statements can be made about educational activities; others that incommensurable and logically different statements can still be validly made. Even if we stress relevance, this is introducing an overt power element into the proceedings, which in effect means that those in positions of power determine what is relevant and those less powerful are silenced. The third strategy suffers from the same problem, which is that it is impossible to reach an agreement about what is good and bad research which can be dissociated from the way that the means for reaching agreement were constructed in the first place.

Fifth, educational discourse is always characterised by reference to the future. The utopian dimension is understood as that which is ideal, both in that it is valued or 'directly committed to the flourishing of education (as an aspect of a wider human flourishing)' (Walsh, 1993, p. 53), and that it excludes considerations of feasibility. Michael Barber (1996), at present the Director of the DfEE's unit on school effectiveness and school improvement, has recently published a book, *The Learning Game*, which may be considered to be utopian. In it, he argues for a reconstruction of teaching and schools. His policy prescriptions include: a professional council for teachers; the need for teaching to become a research-based profession; an

MOT for teachers; a formal apprenticeship for teachers; the creation of a permeable profession; the incorporation of a third-age contribution; target setting for schools; the incorporation of an Individual Learning Promise; the introduction of a Pupil Learning Resource Credit; and so on. We do not need to examine each of these proposals in detail, because what is of interest at the moment is the nature of the theorising that is present. These policy proposals are future-orientated, prescriptive and practical. Barber (1996) also identifies the means by which they could be achieved through a careful manipulation of the policy process. Indeed, what characterises this type of utopian thinking is that it could be made to happen. Barber, himself, in his new role at the DfEE, is now utilising many of these ideas, and though inevitably he is finding that some are more practical than others, he is partly instrumental in turning this vision of his into reality.

What is significant is that his ideas are constitutive of a vision of the future about the way the education service should be constructed, and that they are heavily laden with a particular set of values about the aims and purposes of education. Another utopian thinker, John Dewey (1916, 1933, 1938), though less concerned to describe the way to achieve that utopian vision, was still concerned to describe the values and intended outputs (expressed in terms of the good life) of an education service which did not then exist. Now both Barber is and Dewey was concerned to mount a critique of how the system is and was constructed, but what is significant is that logically their critiques do not and cannot sustain their policy prescriptions. It does not necessarily follow from a diagnosis of low teacher morale that a reprofessionalisation of the teaching profession (in Barber's terms) will lead to improved teacher morale. What these utopian thinkers are doing is making suppositions about the future, based on their knowledge and evaluation of the present. Furthermore, and more fundamentally, what they are seeking to do both through their writings (in the case of Barber and Dewey) and by direct political action (in the case of Barber) is to ensure that their particular value-laden vision of the future comes to fruition. They are not just in the business of predicting the future. Utopian discourse is therefore a means of political persuasion. Education then comprises a set of values which are specifically educative. This book has not sought to describe them, being concerned as it has with epistemological questions about research. However, these educative values are the core of any theorising we may want to do in this field, whether about curriculum-making, the development of research strategies or the identification of aims and purposes for educational activities.

Notes

1 Introduction

1 Goldstein (1998, p. 6) argues that: '. . . it is really quite difficult to provide mathematical models or statistical models which do begin to approach the complexity of the real world, and even when this can be done, the costs of obtaining adequate data to test out these models is very high' and that: 'On the contrary, the use of quantitative methodologies which are rich enough to match the real complexities of the social world may eventually allow us to bridge the gap between qualitative understandings which emphasise these complexities and quantitative tools and understandings which provide formal descriptions of them which can be operated upon to obtain testable predictions, further refinements and useful generalisations.'

2 Tooley with Darby (1998) analysed 41 articles from *The British Journal of Sociology of Education, British Educational Research Journal, British Journal of Educational Studies* and *The Oxford Review of Education* in terms of a number of pre-stated criteria. These criteria were expressed in the form of questions. For empirical research papers the following questions were asked: 1) Is the argument coherent and lucidly expressed? 2) Do the conclusions follow from the premises and argument? 3) Are unfamiliar terms adequately defined and assumptions clearly set out? 4) Are concepts used consistently? 5) Are primary sources used? 6) If empirical propositions are introduced, are references given for these? 7) If controversial empirical and non-empirical propositions are introduced, is their controversy acknowledged? 8) Is the relevant literature adequately surveyed? 9) Is the argument free of partisanship? For non-empirical articles the following questions were asked: 1) Is the work of the 'great' figure critically examined? 2) Does the non-empirical work add significantly to the understanding of the empirical (or historical) work? 3) If empirical (or historical) work undermines the non-empirical position, is this noted? What conclusions are drawn from this? They concluded that 26 of the articles failed to meet these standards and that 'this is disturbing, in particular in terms of the general health of the academic research community and its potential influence in terms of the training and education of future teachers' (ibid., p. 6). As this book shows, these criteria are inadequately conceptualised. They were also interpreted in a highly partisan fashion.

3 They complement the argument in Sayer (1992, pp. 5–6). He argues for: 1) 'The world exists independently of our knowledge of it'; 2) 'our knowledge of that world is fallible and theory-laden'; 3) 'knowledge develops neither wholly

145

continuously . . . nor wholly discontinuously'; 4) 'Objects . . . necessarily have particular causal powers'; 5) 'The world is differentiated and stratified'; 6) 'social phenomena such as actions, texts and institutions are context-dependent'; 7) 'Science or the production of any other kind of knowledge is a social practice'; 8) 'Social science must be critical of its object'.

4 Cf. Scott and Usher (1999).

5 Following Hammersley (1992) I use the term to denote a qualitative orientation to research. This argument is more fully developed in Chapter 4.

PART 1: THEORISING EDUCATIONAL RESEARCH

2 The Contested Nature of Educational Research

6 Hammersley (1995, p. 2) develops his own list of positivistic characteristics: 'that which is taken to be the method of the natural sciences is the only rational source of knowledge; that this method should be applied in social research irrespective of any supposedly distinctive features of social reality; that quantitative measurement and experimental or statistical manipulation of variables are essential, or at least ideal, features of scientific research; that research can and should be concerned with producing accounts which correspond to an independent reality; that scientific knowledge consists of universal laws; and that research should be objective with subjective biases being overcome through commitment to the principle of value neutrality'. He then goes on to suggest that it is logically possible to develop a coherent philosophy which does not embrace all of the above points, but only some. Indeed, the argument in this book is testimony to that. Furthermore, he suggests that positivism itself has become a term of abuse and therefore counter-references to it serve no useful purpose. However, the designation of the four elements by Kolakowski (1972) is not purely arbitrary but refers to a model which though inadequate is still internally coherent; that is, it is perfectly feasible to sustain a belief in phenomenalism, nominalism, a distinction between facts and values and the unity of the scientific method without at the same time contradicting oneself. It is in this sense that it is possible to call it an ideal model and therefore to make reference to it and indeed to critique it.

7 Bhaskar (1991) does not mean to imply by this that objects in the world which exist whether they are known or not do not change their nature, especially if those objects are understood as social discourses, institutions or relations. In the social world our descriptions of objects are always fallible and embedded in particular ways of understanding the world. However, this does not preclude the possibility of real social objects existing in the world, even if they are only relatively stable. Bhaskar is as much concerned to show that naive realism is untenable, as he is to suggest that a form of transcendental realism is possible.

8 Though there are some obvious perverse correlations such as the apparent association between stork and human birth rates in certain parts of Sweden in the nineteenth century, identifying other types and examples of perverse correlations may be more difficult. This is because the association which has been established may seem entirely reasonable.

9 Cf. Scott and Usher (1999).

10 The concept of ideology is used in a number of different ways in the literature. It is used here and subsequently to indicate a group of ideas which are systematically and coherently arranged.

11 My purpose here is philosophical and not sociological or historical. For a sociology or history of many of the ideas expressed in this chapter, see Hammersley (1995).

12 The word 'paradigm' is used in a number of different ways, not least by Kuhn (1971) himself. For instance, Gipps (1994) uses it to refer to different and incommensurable assessment frameworks. A paradigm is used here to refer to an epistemological construction.

3 Educational Knowledge

13 Cf. Giddens (1991).

14 This issue has been addressed in Scott and Usher (1999). For Bryman (1988) no necessary linkage has been established between epistemology and methodology; that is, neither an empirical nor a logical connection has been convincingly shown to exist. However, with regards to the first, I suggest (ibid., p. 63) 'that many researchers have not discussed the epistemological bases of their research or written from a paradigmatic perspective are almost truisms. However, what researchers have done in the past cannot be a guide as to what they will do or should do in the future.' In relation to the second point, the argument suggested in this book posits a logical relationship between the two and indeed between epistemology and ontology. These arguments are in response to Bryman (1988, p. 125) who suggests that: 'the problem with the "ought" view is that it fails to recognise that a whole cluster of considerations are likely to impinge on decisions about methods of data collection'.

15 Cf. Bhaskar (1979, 1989) for a fuller discussion of the arguments which support this.

16 These supra-discourses may be called epistemes (Foucault, 1972) or traditions of thought (Macintyre, 1981).

17 See Note 5.

4 Mathematical Modelling

18 The debate between quantitative and qualitative researchers has been ongoing and fierce for much of the last forty years, with different analysts arguing: that there is a need to move beyond the underlying assumptions made by both sides (cf. Bhaskar, 1989); that we should resolve the duality in the distinction (cf. Hammersley, 1992); that a multi-layered approach should be adopted, whereby 'the use of quantitative data and forms of measurement' should be encouraged 'in order to complement the central core of qualitative analysis' (Layder, 1993, p. 127); or even that a resolution has occurred which has left those believing that it is a meaningful distinction 'on the outer fringes of the methodological debate' (Sammons et al., 1997, p. 8). Scott and Usher (1999) discuss these positions.

19 Giddens (1984, p. 31) argues that: 'The social sciences operate with a double hermeneutic involving two way ties with the actions and institutions of those they study. Sociological observers depend upon lay concepts to generate accurate descriptions of social processes; and agents regularly appropriate themes and concepts of social science within their behaviour, thus potentially changing its character. This . . . inevitably takes it some distance from the "cumulative and uncontested" model that naturalistically-inclined sociologists have in mind.'

20 For a discussion of the difference, see Pawson and Tilley (1997).

21 Cf. Bhaskar (1991); Pawson and Tilley (1997); Sayer (1992); and Archer (1995).

22 There is some suggestion that even the physical sciences do not operate in perfectly closed systems because of evidence of observer effects in experiments.

23 Cf. Gipps and Murphy (1994).

24 Cf. Davie et al. (1972); Barnes and Lucas (1974); Yule and Rutter (1985); Stevenson and Fredman (1990).

25 This is further developed in Scott and Usher (1999).

5 Theory into Practice

26 For Habermas (1974), the term 'scientistic' also indicates that science blinds itself to other forms of knowledge and to other ways of conceptualising the theory–practice relationship.

27 Walsh (1993, p. 44) suggests that this view 'in the name of a poorly understood scientific objectivity would bypass the practitioner and concentrate on "techniques", which it would conceive as measurable inputs to be correlated with measurable learning outcomes'. He also suggests that this form of science does not do justice to the scientific discourse, but is still occasionally used to compare scientific with practice-based knowledge and thus as a result misrepresents the relationship between insider and outsider knowledge. In this chapter I argue that outsider or empirical research is possible (though I would not want to call it scientific), but that it is neither inferior nor superior to practice-based knowledge; and furthermore, that the appropriate relationship between the two cannot be settled by reference to the concept of education but only by properly conducted deliberation about the aims and purposes of education within particular systems and institutions.

28 This perspective corresponds to the view of educational research propounded in this book. The way such knowledge is applied to practice does not necessarily lead to the adoption of a technical-rationality model of the relationship between theory and practice, but it still may do so.

29 See also Carr and Kemmis (1986) who argue that collaborative and deliberative forms of action research as advocated by Elliott (1991) may not produce the expected and desired amount of change in schools because the dialogue and the development of knowledge through that dialogue ignores structural elements (both discursive and non-discursive) within institutions and systems.

30 Cf. Giddens (1984).

31 The concepts of literacy and numeracy are multi-faceted and contested.

32 It is sometimes difficult to distinguish between what is planned and unplanned for two reasons. The first is that there may be consequences which are unexpected and could not have been predicted. The second is that if curriculum planners were asked what they intended at the time, they may confuse what they knew then with what they know now.

33 There is some evidence to suggest that OFSTED's methods and procedures are limited both in a methodological and practical sense, see Maw (1998).

34 Cf. Barber (1996).

35 These traditions are epistemic. However, Macintyre would not want to argue, as Foucault (1980) does, that they refer to particular historical periods.

36 Cf. Scott (1994a).

37 There is some evidence to suggest that schools are concentrating their resources and efforts on that relatively small band of children who may or may not eventually achieve a 'C' grade in GCSE.

38 Cf. Elliott (1998).

39 This hardly does justice to the complex set of relations which exist in the discursive domain. However, it does point to the more proactive stance taken by recent UK governments.

40 Cf. Scott and Usher (1999).

PART 2: DISCIPLINARY KNOWLEDGE

6 School Effectiveness Research

41 See Scott (1997) for a discussion of some of the methodological inadequacies of the discourse.

42 Gray and Reynolds (1996, p. viii) argue in Gray et al. (1996) the following: 'In recent years two simple questions have come to dominate the policy-making agenda. How does one tell a "good" school from a "bad" one? And how does one set about improving them? In this volume leading British researchers in school effectiveness and school improvement explore recent research evidence from their respective perspectives and seek ways of integrating the two "traditions".'

43 This book is about educational research and therefore any proper discussion of the aims and purposes of education will have to wait for some other forum. However, this is not to denigrate such work; indeed, it is to suggest that the construction of educational knowledge comprises in part such a discussion.

44 Cf. Elliott (1998).

45 Systems of appraisal and indeed some aspects of OFSTED inspection give head teachers greater powers over teachers than they have had before. What in part has characterised schools over the last fifteen years has been this transfer of power and authority.

46 In Mortimore and Sammons (1997) it is suggested that I have argued in Scott (1997) that empirical investigation of these matters is unnecessary. This involves a misreading of that chapter.

47 Bourdieu (1989) and Bernstein (1990) define 'field' in different ways both from each other and from me.

7 Education Policy

48 For a more detailed discussion of Foucault's notion of power networks, see Chapter 10.

49 Graham and Tytler (1993) give a number of examples of direct interference by Secretaries of State for Education in the formation of education policy.

50 Chitty (1994, p. 21) quotes Rosenhead (1992, pp. 297–298) to show Mrs Thatcher's idiosyncratic style of policy-making: 'the Policy Unit supplies the prime minister with a radically new policy consistent with her principles and instincts. She then announces this policy in a glare of publicity, thereby establishing a political *fait accompli*. The debate having thus been finessed and forestalled, the relevant Department is left with the job of trying to make the innovation work. As the policy is commonly only in outline form and has not been subject to the filter of critical scrutiny, this task has been known to present some difficulties.' These debates, arguments and idiosyncratic ways of working are mirrored at every stage of the proceedings.

51 Ball (1994, p. 18), for instance, suggests that 'policies *are* textual interventions into practice; and although many teachers (and others) are proactive, "writerly",

readers of texts, their readings and reactions are not constructed in circumstances of their own making. Policies pose problems to their subjects, problems that must be solved in context . . . The point is that we cannot predict or assume how they will be acted on in every case in every setting, or what their immediate effect will be, or what room for manoeuvre actors will find for themselves.'

52 This supports the argument developed in Chapters 2 and 3 that any theory of how the policy process works is necessarily underdeveloped and undertheorised.

53 This argument is more fully developed in the first part of this book.

54 James and Gipps (1998, p. 293) offer a different view to Dearing (1993). They argue that a national assessment system should comprise: 1) 'National tests which assess retention and recall of factual information, and the ability to demonstrate basic skills, should be balanced by more extended assessment tasks which give students an opportunity to demonstrate their ability to apply principles, concepts and higher-order skills in contexts other than those in which they learnt them'; 2) The creation of a bank of assessment tasks; 3) 'All assessment tests and tasks need to be carefully developed, trialed, administered and moderated . . . and to have an acceptable degree of reliability'; 4) A principle of readiness should be built into the system; 5) Profile reports for parents should be created; 6) 'Schools should analyse . . . the full range of their students' achievements so that the relative strengths and weaknesses in different kinds of learning can be evaluated, and test results can be put in their proper context'; 7) Individually ranked league tables of schools should be abolished; 8) 'National monitoring should be based on the results of both short tests and more extended tasks, to represent the full range of learning objectives. To be manageable this should be organized using only a light matrix-sample of students and schools . . . but sufficient to enable reliable generalisations to the system as a whole.'

55 This case study concludes with the publication of the Dearing Report. Inevitably, with the new review of the UK National Curriculum taking place at the time of the publication of this book, new arrangements for assessment will be set in place. My purpose in this chapter has been to reflect on the shifting networks of power and influence which characterised UK educational policy reform in the late 1980s and early 1990s.

8 Biography and Auto-biography

56 This is of course not Mary O'Brien's real name.

9 Researching 'Race' and 'Ethnicity'

57 These debates have become increasingly acrimonious. On the one side are Hammersley (1995, 1998), Hammersley and Gomm (1993) and Foster (1990a, b, 1993); on the other side are Gillborn and Drew (1992), Gillborn (1998), Connolly (1992), Connolly and Troyna (1998) and Troyna (1993).

58 This research was sponsored by *The Voice* newspaper. It investigated the school experiences and career aspirations of African/Caribbean 16–30-year-olds. Data were collected by questionnaire and group interviews. A total of 608 completed questionnaires were received. In addition, a series of group interviews was arranged. These interviews took place in polytechnics, colleges of further education, youth clubs, advice centres, employment centres, health education centres, schools and community colleges.

59 In particular, cf. Gillborn (1998).

60 Cf. Macintyre (1981); indeed, this is central to the argument developed in this book.
61 A distinction is being referred to here between competence and performance (Wood and Power, 1987).
62 Structural properties of institutions compel no-one; however, it is possible to distinguish between loosely constructed arrangements which have not been formalised and institutional arrangements which have been formalised or their dissolution would mean that the institution ceases to function.
63 Cf. Foster et al. (1996).

10 Post-modernism

64 Foucault during his life had profound disagreements with other post-modernist thinkers, such as Derrida. The latter, for example, in 1964 attacked *Histoire de la Folie* in the following terms: 'Foucault's book is a powerful gesture of protection and confinement. A Cartesian gesture for the twentieth century. A recuperation of negativity'; and in a similar vein: 'Foucault is operating according to which everything in the structural totality is bound up together and circular. Structuralist totalitarianism may be effecting an act that confines the cogito, an act which may be of the same type as that of the violence of the classical age. I am not saying that Foucault's book is totalitarian. I am saying that it sometimes runs the risk of being totalitarian.' (Quoted in Macey, 1993.)
65 Foucault borrows from Bentham the notion of the panopticon and the singular way that prisoners, or indeed the population in general, are always conscious of being observed and therefore policed. This means for him a continuous process of surveillance.
66 There is no intention here to suggest that Foucault borrowed the idea from Bhaskar; rather, that the epistemic fallacy and its solution provide a possible way out of his dilemma.
67 Popper (1976, pp. 89–90) sets out his method: 1) Tentative solutions to certain problems should be tried out. Solutions should be proposed and criticised. If a proposed solution is not open to pertinent criticism, it is excluded. 2) An attempt is made to refute it. 3) If this succeeds, another solution is suggested. 4) If it withstands criticism, it is accepted temporarily. 5) Thus this method is one of tentative attempts to solve problems by conjectures which are controlled by severe criticism.
68 Foucault was severely criticised by historians, amongst others, not for using an historical method but for misusing it (Macey, 1993).
69 Taylor (1998, p. 152) writes: 'He dashes the hope, if we had one, that there is some good we can *affirm*, as a result of the understanding that analyses give us. And by the same token, he seems to raise a question whether there is such a thing as a way out. This is rather paradoxical, because Foucault's analyses seem to bring *evils* to light; and yet he wants to distance himself from the suggestion which would seem inescapably to follow, that the negation or overcoming of these evils promotes a good.'
70 Cf. Henriques et al. (1984).
71 If he is merely describing a private morality, then what is the point of writing about it and publishing those writings. The act of dissemination means that it is both perlocutionary and recommendatory.
72 Blacker (1998) certainly defends Foucault in these terms. However, such a defence would seem to negate the point and purpose of Foucault's philosophy.

73 Rorty (1986) suggests that Foucault's viewpoint is ultimately incoherent because he identifies a platform to resist domination and subjugation and at the same time denies that he is holding an explicit normative position.

11 Afterthoughts: Changing Knowledge of Relatively Unchanging Entities

74 Indeed, Bhaskar (1989) sets out a theory of how they change. His notion of transitive knowledge of intransitive entities is an attempt to build in a realist dimension alongside the idea that our attempts at knowing are always context-specific.

75 Cf. Lee (1998).

76 The histories of other fields, especially perhaps foundational disciplines such as Sociology of Education, Philosophy of Education and Psychology of Education, have yet to be written. What would characterise them is how they have become progressively marginalised as dimensions of current educational discourses.

77 Cf. Kysilka (1998).

78 Cf. Adey (1997).

79 Another example is Egan's (1990) stages of human development. He writes: '. . . the process of educational development I have described earlier is a natural process: the sequences of stages I have sketched is a necessary sequence'. He argues that human development can be described in terms of four stages: the mythic, the romantic, the philosophic and the ironic. At the mythic stage, the child seeks absolute accounts of matters in the world and demands precise fixed meanings. The world is not yet understood as autonomous and objective. This stage ultimately gives way to the romantic. The world is now increasingly becoming separate, autonomous, fundamentally different for the child. The immature ego is beginning to evolve and strengthen. The philosophic stage is the first of the adult stages and would seem to characterise much adult thinking in the world. Systems of thought are adopted in relatively crude ways. They are crude because they ignore the particular and fail to describe adequately the complexity of events and activities in the world. The final stage for Egan is the ironic. Full maturity is achieved; one enters into a 'correct' relationship with the world. These and the other schemes described in this chapter all suffer from the delusion that their preferred way of understanding the world is the only one and it is therefore in this sense that it is natural.

References

ADEY, P. (1997) 'Dimensions of progression in a curriculum', *The Curriculum Journal*, **8**, 3, pp. 367–392.

ARCHER, M. (1982) 'Morphogenesis versus structuration', *British Journal of Sociology*, **33**, 4, pp. 455–483.

ARCHER, M. (1988) *Culture and Agency*, Cambridge: Cambridge University Press.

ARCHER, M. (1990) 'Human agency and social structure: A critique of Giddens', in CLARK, J., MODGIL, C. and MODGIL, S. (1990) *Anthony Giddens: Consensus and Controversy*, London: Falmer Press.

ARCHER, M. (1995) *Realist Social Theory: The Morphogenetic Approach*, Cambridge: Cambridge University Press.

AYER, A. J. (1954) *Knowledge, Truth and Logic*, London: Gollancz.

BALL, S. (1982) 'Competition and conflict in the teaching of English: a socio-historical analysis', *Journal of Curriculum Studies*, **15**, 1, pp. 1–28.

BALL, S. (1987) *The Micro-Politics of the School*, London: Methuen.

BALL, S. (1994) *Education Reform: A Critical and Post-structural Approach*, Buckingham: Open University Press.

BALL, S. (1998) 'Educational studies, policy entrepreneurship and social theory', in SLEE, R., TOMLINSON, S. and WEINER, G. (eds.) *School Effectiveness for Whom? Challenges to the School Effectiveness and School Improvement Movements*, London: Falmer Press.

BARBER, M. (1996) *The Learning Game: Arguments for an Education Revolution*, London: Victor Gollanz.

BARNES, J. and LUCAS, H. (1974) 'Positive discrimination in education: individuals, groups and institutions', in LEGGATT, T. (ed.) *Sociological Theory and Survey Research*, London: Sage.

BARTHES, R. (1975) *S/Z*, London: Jonathon Cape.

BEATTIE, A. (1987) *History in Peril*, London: Centre for Policy Studies.

BERNSTEIN, B. (1971) 'On the classification and framing of educational knowledge', in YOUNG, M. (ed.) *Knowledge and Control*, London: Collier-Macmillan.

BERNSTEIN, B. (1985) 'On pedagogic discourse', *Handbook of Theory and Research in the Sociology of Education*, New York: Greenwood Press.

BERNSTEIN, B. (1990) *The Structuring of Pedagogic Discourse*, London: Routledge.

BHASKAR, R. (1979) *Possibility of Naturalism*, London: Harvester Wheatcheaf.

References

BHASKAR, R. (1989) *Reclaiming Reality*, London: Verso.

BHASKAR, R. (1991) *Philosophy and the Idea of Freedom*, Oxford: Blackwell.

BLACKER, D. (1998) 'Intellectuals at work and in power: Towards a Foucaultian research ethic', in POPKEWITZ, T. and BRENNAN, M. (eds.) *Foucault's Challenge: Discourse, Knowledge and Power in Education*, Columbia University: Teachers College Press.

BOURDIEU, P. (1989) *Distinction: A Social Critique of the Judgement of Taste*, London: Routledge.

BOURDIEU, P. and PASSERON, J-C. (1980) *Reproduction*, London: Sage.

BOWE, R., BALL, S. with GOLD, A. (1992) *Reforming Education and Changing Schools: Case Studies in Policy Sociology*, London: Routledge.

BRENNAN, M. (1998) 'Education doctorates: Reconstructing professional partnerships around research?', in LEE, A. and GREEN, B. (eds.) *Postgraduate Studies/Postgraduate Pedagogy*, Sydney: Centre for Language and Literacy, and University Graduate School, University of Technology, Sydney.

BROWN, M. (1992) 'Elaborate nonsense? The muddled tale of standard assessment tasks in mathematics at key stage 3', in GIPPS, C. (ed.) *Developing Assessment for the National Curriculum*, London: Institute of Education, University of London.

BROWN, S., DUFFIELD, J. and RIDDELL, S. (1995) 'School effectiveness research: The policy makers' tool for school improvement', *European Educational Research Association Bulletin*, **1**, 1, pp. 6–15.

BRYMAN, A. (1988) *Quality and Quantity in Social Research*, London: Unwin and Hyman.

CARR, W. and KEMMIS, S. (1986) *Becoming Critical: Education, Knowledge and Action Research*, Lewes: Falmer.

CHERRYHOLMES, C. (1988) 'An exploration of meaning and the dialogue between textbooks and teaching', *Journal of Curriculum Studies*, **20**, 1, pp. 1–21.

CHITTY, C. (1994) 'Consensus to conflict: The structure of educational decision-making transformed', in SCOTT, D. (ed.) *Accountability and Control in Educational Settings*, London: Cassell.

CLARKE, K. (1991) *Department of Education and Science Bulletin*, London: DES.

COLLIER, A. (1994) *Critical Realism: An Introduction to Roy Bhaskar's Philosophy*, London and New York: Verso.

CONNOLLY, P. (1992) 'Playing it by the rules: the politics of research in "race" and education', *British Educational Research Journal*, **18**, 2, pp. 133–148.

CONNOLLY, P. and TROYNA, B. (eds.) (1998) *Researching Race in Education: Politics, Theory and Practice*, Buckingham: Open University Press.

CREEMERS, B. (1994) 'The history, value and purpose of school effectiveness studies', in REYNOLDS, D., CREEMERS, B., NESSELRADT, P., SHAFFER, E., STRINGFIELD, S. and TEDDLIE, C. (eds.) *Advances in School Effectiveness: Research and Practice*, Oxford: Pergamon.

CROSSMAN, R. (1980) 'Do readers make meaning?', in SULLERMAN, S. and CROSSMAN, R. (eds.) *The Reader in the Text: Essays on Audience and Interpretation*, Princeton: Princeton University Press.

DAVIE, R., BUTLER, N. and GOLDSTEIN, H. (1972) *From Birth to Seven*, London: Longman.

DEARING, R. (1993) *The National Curriculum and its Assessment*, London and York: School Examination and Assessment Council and National Curriculum Council.

DEEM, R. (1994) 'School governing bodies – public concerns and private interests', in SCOTT, D. (ed.) *Accountability and Control in Educational Settings*, London: Cassell.

DEPARTMENT OF EDUCATION AND SCIENCE (1988a) *Task Group on Assessment and Testing: A Report*, London: DES.

DEPARTMENT OF EDUCATION AND SCIENCE (1988b) *Three Supplementary Reports to TGAT*, London: DES.

DEWEY, J. (1916) *Democracy and Education*, Toronto: Macmillan.

DEWEY, J. (1933) *How We Think*, New York: Heath.

DEWEY, J. (1938) *Experience and Education*, London: Collier-Macmillan.

DICKINSON, R. and LEE, P. (eds.) (1978) *History Teaching and Historical Understanding*, London: Heinemann Educational.

ECO, V. (1984) *Semiotics and the Philosophy of Language*, Minneapolis: University of Minnesota Press.

EGAN, K. (1990) *Individual Development and the Curriculum*, London: Routledge.

ELLIOTT, J. (1991) *Action Research for Educational Change*, Milton Keynes: Open University Press.

ELLIOTT, J. (1996) 'School effectiveness research and its critics: alternative visions of schooling', *Cambridge Journal of Education*, **26**, 2, pp. 199–224.

ELLIOTT, J. (1998) *The Curriculum Experiment: Meeting the Challenge of Social Change*, Buckingham: Open University Press.

ERBEN, M. (1996) 'The purposes and processes of biographical method', in SCOTT, D. and USHER, R. (eds.) *Understanding Educational Research*, London: Routledge.

ERBEN, M. (1998) 'Introduction', in ERBEN, M. (ed.) *Biography and Education: A Reader*, London: Falmer Press.

EVERS, C. and LAKOMSKI, G. (1991) *Knowing Educational Administration: Contemporary Methodological Controversies in Educational Administration*, Oxford: Pergamon Press.

FIELDING, M. (1997) 'Beyond school effectiveness and school improvement: Lighting the slow fuse of possibility', in WHITE, J. and BARBER, M. (eds.) *Perspectives on School Effectiveness and School Improvement*, Bedford Way Paper, Institute of Education, University of London.

FOGARTY, R. (1991a) *The Mindful School: How to Integrate the Curriculum*, Pallantine, IL: Skylight Publishing.

FOGARTY, R. (1991b) 'Ten ways to integrate the curriculum', *Educational Leadership*, **47**, 2, pp. 61–65.

FOSTER, P. (1990a) *Policy and Practice in Multicultural and Anti-racist Education*, London: Routledge.

FOSTER, P. (1990b) 'Cases not proven: an evaluation of two studies of teacher racism', *British Educational Research Journal*, **16**, 4, pp. 335–348.

FOSTER, P. (1993) 'Teacher attitudes and Afro-Caribbean achievement', *Oxford Review of Education*, **18**, 3, pp. 269–282.

FOSTER, P., GOMM, R. and HAMMERSLEY, M. (1996) *Constructing Educational Inequality*, London: Falmer Press.

FOUCAULT, M. (1972) *The Archeology of Knowledge*, London: Routledge.

References

FOUCAULT, M. (1979) *Discipline and Punish: The Birth of the Prison*, New York: Vintage.

FOUCAULT, M. (1980) *Power/Knowledge*, Brighton: Harvester Press.

FOUCAULT, M. (1983) 'On the genealogy of ethics: An overview of work in progress', in DREYFUS, H. and RABINOW, P. (eds.) *Michael Foucault: Beyond Structuralism and Hermeneutics*, Chicago: University of Chicago Press.

GADAMER, H-G. (1975) *Truth and Method*, London: Sheed and Ward.

GIDDENS, A. (1984) *The Constitution of Society*, Cambridge: Polity Press.

GIDDENS, A. (1991) *Modernity and Self-Identity: Self and Society in the Late Modern Age*, Cambridge: Polity Press.

GILLBORN, D. (1998) 'Racism and the politics of qualitative research: Learning from controversy and critique', in CONNOLLY, P. and TROYNA, B. (eds.) (1998) *Researching Race in Education: Politics, Theory and Practice*, Buckingham: Open University Press.

GILLBORN, D. and DREW, D. (1992) '"Race", class and school effects', *New Community*, **18**, 4, pp. 551–565.

GIPPS, C. (1990) 'National assessment: A comparison of English and American trends', in BROADFOOT, P., MURPHY, R. and TORRANCE, H. (eds.) *Changing Educational Assessment*, London: Routledge.

GIPPS, C. (1994) *Beyond Testing: Towards a Theory of Educational Assessment*, London: Falmer Press.

GIPPS, C. and MURPHY, P. (1994) *A Fair Test? Assessment, Achievement and Equity*, Milton Keynes: Open University Press.

GIROUX, H. (1983) *Theory and Resistance in Education*, London: Heinemann.

GOLDSTEIN, H. (1987) *Multilevel Models in Education and Social Research*, Oxford: Clarendon Press.

GOLDSTEIN, H. (1989) 'Pyschometric test theory and educational assessment', in SIMONS, H. and ELLIOTT, J. (eds.) *Rethinking Appraisal and Assessment*, Milton Keynes: Open University Press.

GOLDSTEIN, H. (1998) *Models for Reality: New Approaches to the Understanding of Educational Processes*, A Professorial Lecture, Institute of Education, University of London.

GOLDSTEIN, H. and MYERS, K. (1997) 'School effectiveness research: A bandwagon, a hijack or a journey towards enlightenment? Paper presented at the British Educational Research Association, 14th August.

GOODSON, I. (1985) (ed.) *Social Histories of the Secondary Curriculum: Subjects for Study*, London and Philadelphia: Falmer Press.

GRAHAM, D. and TYTLER, D. (1993) *A Lesson for us All*, London: Routledge.

GRAY, J. (1991) 'The quality of schooling: frameworks for judgements', *British Journal of Educational Studies*, **38**, 3, pp. 204–233.

GRAY, J., REYNOLDS, D., FITZGIBBON, C. and JESSON, D. (1996) *Merging Traditions: The Future of Research on School Effectiveness and School Improvement*, London: Cassell.

GUBA, E. and LINCOLN, Y. (1985) *Naturalistic Enquiry*, London: Sage.

GUBA, E. and LINCOLN, Y. (1989) *Fourth Generation Evaluation*, London: Sage.

HABERMAS, J. (1974) 'Rationalism divided in two', in GIDDENS, A. (ed.) *Positivism and Sociology*, Aldershot: Gower Publishing Company Ltd.

HABERMAS, J. (1987) *Knowledge and Human Interests*, Cambridge: Polity Press.
HACKING, I. (1981) 'Introduction', in HACKING, I. (ed.) *Scientific Revolutions*, Oxford: Oxford University Press.
HALSEY, C. (1975) 'Sociology and the equality debate', *Oxford Review of Education*, **1**, 1, pp. 9–23.
HAMILTON, D. (1997) 'Peddling feel-good fictions', in WHITE, J. and BARBER, M. (eds.) *Perspectives on School Effectiveness and School Improvement*, Bedford Way Paper, Institute of Education, University of London.
HAMMERSLEY, M. (1992) *What's Wrong with Ethnography?* London: Routledge.
HAMMERSLEY, M. (1995) *The Politics of Social Research*, London: Sage Publications.
HAMMERSLEY, M. (1998) 'Partisanship and credibility: The case of the anti-racist', in CONNOLLY, P. and TROYNA, B. (eds.) (1998) *Researching Race in Education: Politics, Theory and Practice*, Buckingham: Open University Press.
HAMMERSLEY, M. and GOMM, R. (1993) 'A Response to Gillborn and Drew on "race", class and school effects', *New Community*, **19**, 2, pp. 348–353.
HARGREAVES, D. (1996a) *Teaching as a Research-based Profession: Possibilities and Prospects*, The Teacher Training Agency Annual Lecture 1996, mimeo.
HARGREAVES, D. (1996b) 'Educational research and evidence-based educational research: A response to critics', *Research Intelligence*, **58**, November, pp. 12–16.
HARRIS, K. (1979) *Education and Knowledge*, London: Routledge and Kegan Paul.
HATCHER, R. and TROYNA, B. (1994) 'A ball by ball account', *Journal of Education Policy*, **9**, 2, pp. 155–170.
HEIDEGGER, M. (1962) *Being and Time*, Oxford: Basil Blackwell.
HENRIQUES, J., HOLLOWAY, W., URWIN, C., VENN, C. and WALKERDINE, V. (1984) *Changing the Subject: Psychology, Social Regulation and Subjectivity*, London: Methuen.
JAMES, M. and GIPPS, C. (1998) 'Broadening the basis of assessment to prevent the narrowing of learning', *The Curriculum Journal*, **9**, 3, pp. 285–297.
KOGAN, M. (1986) *Educational Accountability: An Analytical Overview*, London: Hutchinson.
KOHLBERG, L. (1976) 'Moral stages and moralization: the cognitive-developmental approach', in LICKONA, T. (ed.) *Moral Development and Behaviour*, London: Holt, Rinehart and Winston.
KOLAKOWSKI, L. (1972) *Positivist Philosophy*, Penguin: Harmondsworth.
KUHN, T. (1971) *The Structure of Scientific Revolutions*, Chicago: University of Chicago Press.
KYSILKA, M. (1998) 'Understanding integrated curriculum', *The Curriculum Journal*, **9**, 2, pp. 197–210.
LAWRENCE, D. (1988) *Enhancing Self-Esteem in the Classroom*, London: Paul Chapman.
LAWTON, D. (1992) 'Whatever happened to the TGAT Report', in GIPPS, C. (ed.) *Developing Assessment for the National Curriculum*, Institute of Education, University of London.
LAYDER, D. (1993) *New Strategies in Social Research*, Cambridge: Polity Press.
LEE, A. (1998) 'Research and knowledge in the professional doctorate', Paper presented at Symposium: *Professional Doctorates in New Times for the Australian University*, AARE, Brisbane, December 1997.

References

LEVINE, D. (1992) 'An interpretive review of US research and practice dealing with unusually effective schools', in REYNOLDS, D. and CUTTANCE, P. (eds.) *School Effectiveness Research, Policy and Practice*, London: Cassell.

LEVINE, D. and LEZOTTE, L. (1990) *Unusually Effective Schools: A Review and Analysis of Research and Practice*, Madison, WI: National Centre for Effective Schools: Research and Development.

MACEY, D. (1993) *The Lives of Michael Foucault*, London: Hutchinson.

MACGREGOR, J. (1990) *Speeches on Education: National Curriculum and Assessment*, London: DES.

MACINTYRE, A. (1981) *After Virtue: A Study in Moral Theory*, London: Duckworth.

MACINTYRE, A. (1988) *Whose Justice? Which Rationality?* London: Duckworth.

MARENBON, J. (1987) *English, Our English*, London: Centre for Policy Studies.

MAW, J. (1998) 'An inspector speaks: The annual report of Her Majesty's Chief Inspector of Schools', *The Curriculum Journal*, 9, 2, pp. 145–152.

MORTIMORE, P. (1992) 'Issues in school effectiveness', in REYNOLDS, D. and CUTTANCE, P. (eds.) *School Effectiveness Research, Policy and Practice*, London: Cassell.

MORTIMORE, P. and SAMMONS, P. (1997) 'Endpiece: A welcome and riposte to critics', in BARBER, M. and WHITE, J. (eds.) *Perspectives on School Effectiveness and School Improvement*, Bedford Way Papers, Institute of Education, University of London.

MORTIMORE, P., SAMMONS, P. and HILLMAN, J. (1997) 'Key characteristics of effective schools: A response to "peddling feel-good fictions"' in WHITE, J. and BARBER, M. (eds.) *Perspectives on School Effectiveness and School Improvement*, Bedford Way Paper, Institute of Education, University of London.

MORTIMORE, P., SAMMONS, P., STOLL, L., LEWIS, D. and ECOB, R. (1988) *School Matters: The Junior Years*, Wells: Open Books.

NORTH, J. (1987) *GCSE: An Introduction*, London: Claridge Press.

NOSS, R., GOLDSTEIN, H. and HOYLES, C. (1989) 'Graded assessment and learning hierarchies in mathematics', *British Educational Research Journal*, 15, 2, pp. 109–120.

NUTTALL, D. (1995) 'Reliability in educational assessments', in MURPHY, R. and BROADFOOT, P. (eds.) *Effective Assessment and the Improvement of Education: A Tribute to Desmond Nuttall*, London: Falmer Press.

OFSTED (1996) *The Teaching of Reading in 45 London Primary Schools*, London: HMSO.

O'HEAR, A. (1987) 'The GCSE philosophy of education', in NORTH, J. (ed.) *GCSE: An Introduction*, London: Claridge Press.

OUTHWAITE, W. (1990) 'Outhwaite replies to Archer', in CLARK, J., MODGIL, C. and MODGIL, S. (1990) *Anthony Giddens: Consensus and Controversy*, London: Falmer Press.

PAWSON, R. and TILLEY, N. (1997) *Realistic Evaluation*, London: Sage Publications.

PENNEY, D. and EVANS, J. (1994) 'From "policy" to "practice": The development and implementation of National Curriculum for physical education', in SCOTT, D. (ed.) *Accountability and Control in Educational Settings*, London: Cassell.

PHILLIPS, D. (1993) 'Subjectivity and objectivity: An objective inquiry', in HAMMERSLEY, M. (ed.) *Educational Research: Current Issues*, London: Paul Chapman.

PIAGET, J. (1971) *The Science of Education and the Psychology of the Child*, London: Routledge and Kegan Paul.

POPPER, K. (1976) 'The logic of the social sciences', in ADORNO, T. et al., *The Positivist Dispute in German Sociology*, London: Heinemann.

REYNOLDS, D. (1985) 'The effective school', *Times Educational Supplement*, **20**, September, p. 25.

RICOEUR, P. (1984) *Time and Narrative, Part One*, Chicago: University of Chicago Press.

RICOEUR, P. (1985) *Time and Narrative, Part Two*, Chicago: University of Chicago Press.

RICOEUR, P. (1986) *Time and Narrative, Part Three*, Chicago: University of Chicago Press.

ROGERS, C. (1967) *On Becoming a Person*, London: Constable.

ROGERS, C. (1983) *Freedom to Learn for the 80s*, Columbus, Ohio: Charles E. Merrill Publishing Company.

RORTY, R. (1980) *Philosophy and the Mirror of Nature*, Oxford: Blackwell.

RORTY, R. (1986) 'Foucault and epistemology', in HOY, D. (ed.) *Foucault: A Critical Reader*, Oxford, United Kingdom, and Cambridge, United States of America: Blackwell.

ROSENHEAD, J. (1992) 'Into the swamp: the analysis of social issues', *Journal of the Operational Research Society*, **43**, 4, pp. 293–305.

SAMMONS, P. and REYNOLDS, D. (1997) 'A partisan evaluation – John Elliott on school effectiveness', *Cambridge Journal of Education*, **27**, p. 1.

SAMMONS, P., HILLMAN, J. and MORTIMORE, P. (1995) *Key Characteristics of Effectiveness: A Review of School Effectiveness Research*, London: Office for Standards in Education.

SAMMONS, P., THOMAS, S. and MORTIMORE, P. (1997) *Forging Links: Effective Schools and Effective Departments*, London: Paul Chapman Publishing Ltd.

SAYER, A. (1992) *Method in Social Science*, London: Routledge.

SCHEERENS, J. (1992) *Effective Schooling: Research, Theory and Practice*, London: Cassell.

SCHON, D. (1983) *The Reflective Practitioner: How Professionals Think in Action*, Aldershot: Avebury.

SCHOOLS EXAMINATIONS AND ASSESSMENT COUNCIL (1989a) *National Curriculum Assessment Arrangements (1)*, London: SEAC.

SCHOOLS EXAMINATIONS AND ASSESSMENT COUNCIL (1989b) *National Curriculum Assessment Arrangements (2)*, London: SEAC.

SCOTT, D. (1990) *School Experiences and Career Aspirations of African-Caribbean 16–30 Year Olds*, Centre for Educational Development, Appraisal and Research, University of Warwick.

SCOTT, D. (1991) 'Issues and themes: coursework and coursework assessment in the GCSE', *Research Papers in Education*, **6**, 1, pp. 3–20.

SCOTT, D. (ed.) (1994a) *Accountability and Control in Educational Settings*, London: Cassell.

References

Scott, D. (1994b) 'Making schools accountable: Assessment policy and the Education Reform Act' in Scott, D. (ed.) *Accountability and Control in Educational Settings*, London: Cassell.

Scott, D. (1996) 'Education policy: The secondary phase, *Journal of Education Policy*, **11**, 1, pp. 133–140.

Scott, D. (1997) 'The missing hermeneutical dimension in mathematical modelling of school effectiveness', in White, J. and Barber, M. (eds.) *Perspectives on School Effectiveness and School Improvement*, Bedford Way Paper, Institute of Education, University of London.

Scott, D. (1998) 'Fragments of a life: Recursive dilemmas', in Erben, M. (ed.) *Biography and Education: A Reader*, London: Falmer Press.

Scott, D. (1999) 'Endpiece', in Scott, D. (ed.) *Values and Educational Research*, Bedford Way Paper, Institute of Education, University of London.

Scott, D. and Usher, R. (1999) *Researching Education: Data, Methods and Theory in Educational Enquiry*, London: Cassell.

Self-Esteem Network (1997) *The Self-Esteem Directory*, Dover: Smallwood Publishing.

Shulman, L. (1987) 'Knowledge and teaching: foundations of the new reform', *Harvard Educational Review*, **57**, 1, pp. 1–22.

Smyth, J. (1993) *A Socially Critical View of the Self-managing School*, London: Falmer Press.

Spradberry, J. (1976) 'Conservative pupils? Pupil resistance to curriculum innovation in mathematics', in Whitty, G. and Young, M. F. D. (eds.) *Explorations in the Politics of School Knowledge*, Driffield: Nafferton.

Stevenson, J. and Fredman, G. (1990) 'The social environmental correlates of reading ability', *Journal of Child Psychology and Psychiatry*, **31**, 5, pp. 681–698.

Stronach, I. and MacLure, M. (1997) *Educational Research Undone: The Postmodern Embrace*, Buckingham: Open University Press.

Taylor, C. (1998) 'Foucault on freedom and truth', in Taylor, C. *Philosophical Papers 2*, Cambridge: Cambridge University Press.

Tooley, J. with Darby, D. (1998) *Educational Research: A Critique*, London: Office for Standards in Education.

Troyna, B. (1993) 'Underachiever or misunderstood: a reply to Roger Gomm', *British Educational Research Journal*, **19**, 2, pp. 167–174.

Usher, R. (1996) 'A critique of the neglected assumptions of educational research', in Scott, D. and Usher, R. (eds.) *Understanding Educational Research*, London: Routledge.

Usher, R. (1997) 'Telling a story about research and research as story-telling: Post modern approaches to social research', in McKenzie, G., Powell, J. and Usher, R. (eds.) *Understanding Social Research: Perspectives on Methodology and Practice*, London: Falmer Press.

Usher, R., Bryant, I. and Johnstone, R. (1996) *Adult Education and the Postmodern Challenge: Learning Beyond the Limits*, London: Routledge.

Vygotsky, L. S. (1978) *Mind in Society*, Cambridge, Mass: MIT Press.

Walsh, P. (1993) *Education and Meaning: Philosophy in Practice*, London: Cassell.

Weber, M. (1974) 'Subjectivity and determinism', in Giddens, A. (ed.) *Positivism and Sociology*, London: Heinemann Educational Books.

WEINER, G. (1990) 'The framing of school knowledge: History in the National Curriculum', Paper given at the British Educational Research Association Conference, Roehampton College, London, August.

WEXLER, P. (1982) 'Structure, text and subject: A critical sociology of school knowledge', in APPLE, M. (ed.) *Cultural and Economic Reproduction in Education*, London: Routledge and Kegan Paul.

WHITE, J. (1997) 'Philosophical perspectives on school effectiveness and school improvement', in WHITE, J. and BARBER, M. (eds.) *Perspectives on School Effectiveness and School Improvement*, Bedford Way Paper, Institute of Education, University of London.

WILLIS, P. (1977) *Learning to Labour*, Farnborough: Saxon House.

WILSON, R. (1990) 'Sociology and the mathematical method', in GIDDENS, A. and TURNER, J. (eds.) *Social Theory Today*, London: Polity Press.

WOOD, D. (1990) *Philosophy at the Limit*, London: Unwin Hyman.

WOOD, R. and POWER, C. (1987) 'Aspects of the competence-performance distinction: Educational, psychological and measurement issues', *Journal of Curriculum Studies*, **19**, 5, pp. 409–424.

WOODHEAD, C. (1998) 'Foreword', in TOOLEY, J. and DARBY, J. *Educational Research: A Critique*, London: OFSTED.

WORTHEN, J. (1987) 'English', in NORTH, J. (ed.) *GCSE: An Introduction*, London: Claridge Press.

YEATMAN, A. (1990) *Bureaucrats, Technocrats, Femocrats: Essays on the Contemporary Australian State*, Sydney: Allen and Unwin.

YULE, W. and RUTTER, M. (1985) 'Reading and other difficulties', in RUTTER, M. and HERSOV, L. (eds.) *Child and Adolescent Psychiatry: Modern Approaches*, 2nd Edition, Oxford: Blackwell Scientific.

Author index

Adey, P. 139, 152
Archer, M. 3, 28–31, 77, 80–1, 125, 147

Ball, S. 66–7, 81, 149–50
Barber, M. 1, 143–4, 148
Barnes, J. 148
Barthes, R. 79, 90
Beattie, A. 90
Bernstein, B. 76, 79, 137–41, 149
Bhaskar, R. 1, 12–15, 34, 45, 81, 98, 123–5, 132, 146, 147, 152
Blacker, D. 127–8, 151
Bourdieu, P. 44, 68, 149
Bowe, R. 76, 78–9
Brennan, M. 134
Brown, M. 88, 91
Brown, S., 66
Bryman, A. 29, 147
Burgess, R.G. vii

Carr, W. 148
Cherryholmes, C. 79
Chitty, C. 149
Clarke, K. 90–1
Collier, A. 15
Connolly, P. 150
Creemers, B. 64
Crossman, R. 78

Darby, D. 1, 145
Davie, R., 148
Dearing, R. 78, 86, 92–3, 150
Deem, R. 84
Department of Education and Science 85–6, 87–8, 93

Derrida, J. 98
Dewey, J. 144
Dickinson, A. 140–1
Drew, D. 150

Eco, V. 78
Egan, K. 151
Elliott, J. 51, 68, 71, 148, 149
Erben, M. 95, 99, 101
Evans, J. 79
Evers, C. 4

Fielding, M. 70–1
Fogarty, R. 137–9
Foster, P. 112, 117, 150–1
Foucault, M. 4, 7, 20, 75–6, 121–31, 147–8
Fredman, G. 148

Gadamer, H-G. 5, 18, 24–5, 73, 109
Giddens, A. 14, 28–31, 33–4, 39, 80–3, 99, 132–3, 147–8
Gillborn, D. 117, 120, 133, 150
Gipps, C. 41, 47, 91, 93, 147–8, 150
Giroux, H. 78
Goldstein, H. 1, 42, 47, 64, 67–8, 70, 72, 86, 145
Gomm, R. 150
Goodson, I. 81
Graham, D. 76, 149
Gray, J. 63, 67, 149
Guba, E. 3

Habermas, J. 49, 58–9, 119, 148
Hacking, I. 19–20
Halsey, C. 83

Subject index